D1641542

ITS ALL A PROCESS

© 2022 CRECHE SHAW

Paperback ISBN: 978-1-66785-625-4

eBook ISBN: 978-1-66785-626-1

Its All A Process

MY PROCESS MAY HELP YOU ALONG THE WAY

CRECHE

CONTENTS

HEALING

It is a process that cannot be denied.

It is a process that you cannot go tell to hide.

It is a process that you definitely need.

It is a process that will be remembered.

It is a process that is near and tender.

It is a process that is between you and God.

It is a process that is sent to you from above.

It is a process that you had to trust.

It is a process that is so true.

So, trust your heart, you will make it through.

LAUGHING

Why do you laugh? Was it very funny? Was it because you won some money? If you did, Congratulations, I would be laughing with the largest loudest laugh too. Well, we make these sounds from our mouths and they sound cool. However, some laughs sound crazy, silly, creepy, and or super loud; but without a doubt when you hear a good genuine laugh it may make you smile.

COMPANION

(while looking at my granny)

We all need someone around to talk to and to just be near. Sometimes words can make the situation so dear. Sometimes all someone needs is a hug. No one ever knows how long it has been since love was sent. So, maybe it is your turn to give someone a love gift, you may just change their day. Love is very powerful they say. Some are afraid to love but it's not that scary. Just checking up on one is a small gesture of being a friend. It shows you care, the world needs love forever; so the people will slowly change how they feel. We all have been slowly taken away from the real. Desensitized is the word, but I'm the little blue bird that still exist.; that puts words in the air and it hits your ear in the midst. The midst of the day, come on let's play. Play a sweet song, call a friend and remanence over good times. Hug your parent or a pet, it is all love so just think of which way you want to show your love to a companion.

CLOSE

Will we always be around? Around the corner to be there so fast. Fast as the day goes by, all I saw was light; light then turned to midnight sky. Time surely moves swiftly and before we know it, it is on to the next moment in time. Time that we cannot get back in fact it seems that it really is all a dream. Dream up beauty, dream up life on a cloud without ever coming down. Dream that one day we could really all be so close to one another in peace and harmony, one sweet day; if only it would come sooner than later, I will keep dreaming. Come along anyone on this dream with me, don't leave me hanging out there alone. Alone is never what we want, we all want to be close to someone, whether dear to you or not, a close friend or not. Sometimes people will really do anything to keep you from feeling blue. Blue is a great color and it has a lot of meaning. What do you think of when you hear the word blue. I think of the birds and the bees and all that fly in the blue sky. Birds being them, sitting pretty and blue like summer kisses all while wearing those special blue jeans. Oohhh Wee how we all remember those blue jeans that hugged our hips and those sweet kisses that kept us smiling all the way to our sweet dreams. So, keep dreaming and keep them close and then find yourself around the corner the next day telling your best friend all the way to the store all that you did so you won't get bored with your day. Keep your friends close and around so they can always feel like they are in the know because one day they may not be so close.

MEMORIES

We all have these fond times in our lives. Times that made us smile, cry, and even stop and pull up some old photos, an old book, or even step on a ladder to reach in the very back area of the shelf. In the back of the shelf is a very special treasure piece that you hold dear to your heart and only you and a selected few know what was made especially for you. Life is full of these moments and boy I love most of mine. I surely hope that you have also had great times to say the same. I love poetry I love music I love the soul mane. I am here to share a piece of me with you. This is my soul purpose from me to you and trust me when I say you while reading this book you are experiencing a lot of my soon to be memories.

PLAYFULNESS

How much of life do you take seriously? Well not much for me. I could never understand why, and I am not living a lie. I guess it is because I feel like I would be living under a rug if I had to be serious all the time. No room to move just under the rug waiting on the broom. That would be my excitement getting cleaned and shook up like lightening. Forgive me when I say I like being this way. I am a grown woman that loves the lighter side to things. Let us smile, let us sing, let us be merry and free you see I think anything just not to be put back under the rug or stuck in a tree. Even though that sounds really cool and all because I love being in nature but where is the fun in that? Fun is what we are suppose to make of it, not yoga time. Although, yoga is splendid, to do such poses and sit in tranquil spaces but if I cannot run and jump I really don't know how much fun I am really going to have, but the idea is kind of cool. When you have children that are young, You stay young as well, well, only if you have fun and play right along or alongside them. That is the golden rule to saying young, having the right amount of playfulness within.

MOVE

I just cannot seem to keep still, I guess because I am alive. So no Sitting still for me, on the move my body will continue to be in motion. Just like time, I promise, it never stops, I am always busy with something to do. I am kept on my toes and my fingers, arms and legs also get to join in on the fun. I sometimes wish I could just take a break from it all and just rest for about a week or two.But really??? Who will make everything work and continue its great flow if I stop? My world would definitely fall apart if I decide to rest for a week or two. And all of my children will be crying because they would have to do it all on their own. Slow motion has never been me, sometimes as a mom I rarely have time to use the bathroom. My bad to be so honest but it's the truth, and I know many can relate. So, I say what I say and the rest is up to you and how you take in my words. Just like right at this moment while writing, I am being moved to go and pick up my other child (nephew) and my son from the movies, before curfew. So, I got to move fast and flow on this freeway and I shall continue where I left off sometime later whenever I'M MOVED!!

FAITH

If you move by faith you walk a walk that some don't even know about. Some wonder why and some wonder how, well when you stop trying to be perfect with all of your dealings and handlings with life you pretty much have crossed over. Walking by faith is more than a belief it takes real courage and strength to just let go of all preconceived notions and just let God, The Universe, or the spirits around you coordinate your day. Naturally you have a small percentage of guidance with your day but you don't know the outcome and or response of the world around you. I Love God with all of my heart and I have made a lot of bad decisions in my life and still during all of my bad moves I had faith that I would come out on the other side. Survive basically and he never left my side, I have everyday circumstances and I always just have the faith to keep going with no concerns, for I feel that everything will turn out great and if not great, half way and surely okay. Life is too short to worry, so why stress, just keep the faith and life will be just fine. God is Great, God is Good and a Lil Faith Never Hurt Nobody....1LV

REWIND

What do you remember from you past? I thought I had it all Packed and stashed in my mind, but some things have been left behind. If I could go back into time to relive some special moments; like a few good birthdays or special overnighters. I would definitely without a doubt remember all of the good ol' days with granny and grampy. When you could hop in the bed with them and not get looked at like you bumped your head. The days when things were simple and cute, oh how I wish we could just hop in a time machine and see those special times again. Look at me throwing them in my rhyme again. The Good ol' days Thank God for our brains that are so cool and can go into the past. For we cannot rewind and don't have time machines and that is okay my mind will do. Just sit back and think back when you were 10. Rewind the years and Enjoy.

HURT

Pain is excruciating and hurt is almost about the same except that I use hurt for my feelings more. It is a feeling that gets stored deep down under your heart and when it comes up to the front, Oh how you feel it. Your heart actually becomes heavy like a rock. Maybe because it is turning to stone or maybe even black. It feels like you are dying it is so dam heavy, It feels like you just want to stop whatever it is you are doing. Hurt in the heart is not a ride in the park, it's more like someone ran over it. More than likely that is exactly what happened someone ran right over it picked it up and threw it at a tree. Getting over hurt is not the easiest thing to do but with your inner strength trust me you will pull through. Don't let the hurt control you or pull you all the way down and don't go and hurt others to make yourself feel better, because remember just how bad you felt, do you really want that new kind of pain in your chest?

LESSONS

Life surely gives us lessons, everyday there is a lesson or two in it. You may learn something new if you pay attention to the people and things around you. Life is full of lessons or life is a lesson, whichever way you look at it. Time and age allows one to look at life in this manner. If you are fortunate from unfortunate circumstances hopefully you learned from it so the same thing doesn't happen twice or thrice. We are not perfect but luckily we have these not so perfect moments in our lives. How else would we learn and have so many different stories to share with one another since we are all connected and learn from one another, so why not learn to share our ups and downs more. So others can pick up some pointers on life and maybe you may save them from a pitfall or disappointing time. But, ultimately most people still end up doing whatever their heart tells them and if it ends up being that they end up in sorrow of a situation they now have experienced the lesson for themselves and can go back and tell their friends, "You know you were right but I learned my LESSON!"

TIMELESS

Birthdays come every year and each year we get older. We are happy that we got that far in life but it seems as if life is really timeless when you are young. We definitely grow up and time moves for real and it moves faster and faster. It moves so fast it seems to not really matter. Timeless energy, especially when you age, but don't feel that you have aged much. I have seemed to fall into that timeless energy. It feels like time has not moved fast for me but all I know is that I have aged and I have children and shoot they are all aging fast. Where did this time go? I want to be young forever, certainly and I pray that I stay looking young for the rest of my life. I have decided to stay in my timeless energy and stay young since I feel young in time. I suppose I will look old one day. But until then.. I'M YOUNG AND LOST IN TIME.

HAPPINESS

Don't worry now be happy now, Life is too short to feel like you are in a rut. Get out of it, really take a deep breath and climb on up and out of it. Put a happy smile on in your day, it really does feel good. I'm not saying big and wide were it looks like you are faking it or like you are sitting on a cloud and the cloud is cool to sit on and all as I smile so big while typing that sentence to where you could see my whole top row of shiners!! Sitting on a cloud is a good thing and it will make you smile. However, you get my drift, and that word drift sure takes me back to my childhood. That was a word that my parents and grandparents would use often. It was used to make sure they were understood after they said something. You see I love to write, why you ask? It brings me happiness and joy. I also have a lot to say and share, so knowing that I can help someone with words that makes me feel good. Have you ever been so happy that you began to cry? That is how happy I am at this time, and to even share that literally in this space and time with you as I write these words for us all or whomever gets to read, is pure joy. I got so happy because it is my time to shine, to write, and in that moment of writing the simple word DRIFT, I had short memories of my aging parents and of times that once were. So, to be able to pull up good memories just from writing a short piece of inspiration is surely something that is exciting for me. Now my life is calling for a small thing called a shower which is another great form of Happiness.

1ST OF JULY 2019

Busy, Busy, Busy that would be my day from the moment I woke up, every minute I mean Literally!!, I mean like YO…REALLY!! I went to the grocery store before I even made breakfast, then back to the house. I also went to the gas station before returning home. So, After I got home and made breakfast for everybody which includes my eldest son my granny my two nieces and myself. I now am off to cleaning up my Grandma and getting her fed. I then will have a small amount of time to rest my head!! SYKE!! I love to play and so I wish, I could Really get that nap. But seriously, on to the next thing, a trip to three stores with my lil' young princess and her little cousin. After the trips and get us back home again I have to now wash one of my twins hair. Off to the shower now, and yes, now I'm clean finally! So now it's about 1pm and it is lunchtime and after making lunch I now need to start on my nieces hair. After I finish vacuuming up her hair off the floor I take her and her sister home. So, while in motion my son ask me, "Mom, can I just stay?" "Stay!!, How do you even know you can stay, did you ask?" "Where are your clothes?" Was my response. Huh, what? Were my mind thoughts. So, he says, "Well, I'm about to ask my uncle." And I say, "ohhh, okay." Whatever you say young one, were my mind thoughts once again. OH and it continues just like a book that could be made into a motion picture. I Love describing my day and this was just half of it. If only I had all the energy and time to write what happens in the rest of it. One day I may take on the challenge. July 1st 2019 and beyond!!

BRIELLE

(My 7 yr old niece taking a shot a writing in my journal)

This morning was good until my cousin left. Then I played with her. We stopped playing and I went in the kichen (baby typo) with her then she left. But she is come back, tomorrow. And she is going to be her (baby typo) for the Forth(baby typo) of July. Every year she not hear (baby typo) accept (baby typo) for this year. I don't know about my other cousin. Sometimes they come at the end of the fireworks that means the grand finale. But we spend a night at are (baby typo) grandmas house every year. One time are (baby typo) grandma go to the firework place or one year my parent go to the firework place. When she told me she is staying I was happy, I was with joy. Then I told my parents that she was staying for the Forth(baby typo) of July!

ECLIPSE

New beginnings, although, I didn't see the full solar eclipse because of where I live and it is quite okay but I feel the change in the energy. I feel so full of life but stuck slightly in a rut. Although, I am rebirthing myself by freeing myself from my dull, played out marriage and getting a divorce. Unfortunately, but, Fortunately, I have a choice and I tried over a dozen times to repair the wounds but all of my efforts did not make a real difference. So, my eclipse is about to really begin but I am at a stand still kind of sort of because everything that is needed to move forward requires money. So, it is requiring patience. I have so much of it, but it hurts because I am anxious to move along and not have the patience right now. I have to embrace the change that is coming for me but be willing to accept my bit of a rut feeling and situation. I know that it is only temporary, and that is what I must remember. Now, as for all of this being understood that is an understatement. It is my life, of course I understand it. I live it!! Good Lord keep me sane and hold me close because everything is tempting. Nothing bad, just to escape but that can be dangerous . No lie, so, I will stay low key and let the pages turn as slowly as they may and I will continue to flip with the pages and just continue to be still and wait for the day I will see the next Eclipse.

ESCAPE

How fast can you get out of a sticky situation? Or simply how fast can you run? I can run pretty fast and Thank God for that. Also my brain is pretty fast too which accurately allows me to process information, which could also help me get out of a situation that I may just not want to be in and or around. Yes, today well more like late evening I am taking a walk and was approaching my neighborhood and I cross the light there is a man in the turning lane and he ask from his car if I needed a ride. I ignore him because its late and I don't like attention in that manner. So, what does he do he makes a u turn once he turns left to come back to harass me. So, I stop immediately and turn back the other way I was walking and in the direction that he wanted to go in originally. I pause to see what he did and he turned Luckily, I was in my neighborhood and knew all of the streets and where all streets turn, dead ends, brick walls to hide behind and alleyways if need be. My life literally just turned into a motion picture. However, I turned back around and went to the first street he turned left on and I sat behind a car.. He went seven houses down and turned left again. Now if he knew the neighborhood that well he would have turned left again to come back out to the main street he was just about to pass before he made an u -turn. So, once I saw him make the left eventually I ran into my neighborhood and took my first right down a street that he would not look down because once he got back to that original spot we were at hopefully he would have sense enough to see that I'm not there. I had enough sense to get the hell out of there. I cannot believe my night, took a night walk and look what came my way. Another Invasion of my Space But Guess What?.. I Escaped!!!

SOUND

As a song gets finished on the radio app that I'm listening too and the sound that I'm searching for is always a soulful sound and believe me there are plenty of pleasing sounds and some that are not and maybe quite annoying but all the sounds send out signals and vibes throughout the day, night and all through the universe. I love sounds, preferably good music or some good lyricists. I can just listen to nature also, it actually is the best, pure sounds of nature. Birds, wind, and trees; Yes, trees! Yes, they make sounds or speak sometimes. However, embrace the sounds in your day!!

PEACE

Keep the peace, stay positive and keep moving forward. Don't look back and don't worry about anything. Just do you and keep an open mind to all of the day and to all the things around you. Love long and Love always. Peace and Blessings to All and Pray for the World and Peace I pray we can all reach World Peace..1LV

KIMANI'S ENTRY

(My baby girls first entry for mom)

Today was fun but kinda (baby typo) dumb. I went away for only one day. And now I (baby typo) back to play at home with my family. Pleasant day, good day, sun is shining, trees are blowing grass is greeny(baby made up word) my brother is being a big meanie. My Scorpio gang is always ready to play the game (me my bro and Londin) My little cuzin(baby typo) my best friend is always with me and I love her to.(baby typo) As soon as I go to sleep Sticks comes in my room door and I can't forget about him because there is six of us.

4TH OF JULY

Bang, Bang, Pow, that is all you hear in the air once night falls. All night into the next day because it's almost midnight and I still hear them loud and clear our Finale was done at 10:34 that was an early night for us for the first time ever. Although it ended early it was an excellent ending and that was what was up!! Yes, we did it big and it was done right. Well thanks to my mother, she makes it a yearly tradition to go a few months early. She takes a 4 hour trip just to excite and to also outdo all the neighbors. Oh so exciting it can be. All of the children going nutty, left and right they go. They are all hyped up on soda and candy; racing one another and having a blast. Since this day only comes around once a year they make the best of the night. The night was nice and sweet and one last thing. R.I.P to one of my old friends, he was surely there with us in spirit. He lived on my street and his birthday is on the 4^{th,} so we lit it up Indeed!! Happy 4th!!

MONDAY NIGHT

Pick up my pen and I'm ready to go. Ready to write. Ready to flow. The vibe is high and I feel oh so alive. Although I have not written in four days I want to make up for my lack of. I even took a pass on a midnight or evening walk. It's not quite midnight but by the time I'd return to my destination midnight it surely will be. Oh how wonderful it all is, the paper and this pen with the ink that flows on from the mere thoughts running through my mind; like the famous saying, "Their mouths run like a water faucet." Yep, that's me, much to say and I can do it efficiently. Just let me keep flowing to you, just what I'm here to do. Infinity, that's the number of the day and if you want to go a little into the time its not two thousand and nine. We a whole decade past that on the 8th day and prayfully we all see the day after we read this. I was born over three decades ago and I feel that time is moving fast everyday. So, move with the flow of the wind in the day and try to put your best vibe forward. Be true to self and appreciate the good efforts from others. Time is everything, It's Fluid, Move with it and Enjoy Every Minute.

ANTICIPATION

Cravings, appetites, wants, needs, and just the thought process of anticipation. Knowing about something is definitely all the reason why anticipation happens anyways. If it was something craved like a sweet treat out by the pier at a little stand that isn't there anymore. You didn't anticipate any of that to happen after you paid for parking and walked eight blocks from the car. Also by them not being there the craving wasn't fulfilled. Now you have to locate a new sweet treat location. All the rules to the things that we expect to go accordingly, Just don't have an expectation. Just learn to go with the flow. I try my hardest to use that concept to my every exchange in everyday life. And I know that can be a little difficult. Although, I have not always been like this. I feel that I need to think about concepts, subjects, and content matters of the Heart and souuuuul. ONELV

ENERGY

Feel the energy and roll with me. Right now I hear fireworks but I listen more closely and although they have stopped I wonder if it really was a firework or was it a few gun shots. I really cannot tell but luckily it has really gone away for a cool little while now and I'm feeling the way I am feeling all while the time is passing on by, its not midnight yet and when it is I will stop and pick it up later on in the day. Airplanes are moving flying up above me in the air and I really can not say that I really want to fly right at this time. Nothing against the pilot or anything. I'm just a little not entrusting in the whole flying culture. It is a big exchange of energy on, in and around the airport areas not saying anything bad, I'm just saying talk about energy. That's a lot and that whole experience of flying has me in my feelings and trying to control my energy around all of the different energy all while being a little nervous due to the fact that I don't really care for heights!! There is a lot of different emotions that I have that are attached to this here topic of flying, airports, and all that Energy!!

IT'S BEEN SOME TIME

(My Lyrics to a melody)

Yes, it's been a while

I pray that you've been well, I have so much to talk to you about. Please hear me I've been thinking about you all day. (2x) About you and me, Yeah Baby can you hear me? I'm crying out to you. You may not believe me but I cant stop thinking about you. On my mind daily, thinking that I may be going crazy. Stuck thinking bout you. What I'm gonna do. OHHHH Baby krazy thinking of you. Tell me why it has been so long? I thought that we were really past all that silly back and forth so I thought that I would call you to see where we stand, maybe we could be just like we planned. I don't know what happened to us but I think we might as well just make up.. Yeah it's been a long time Melody:(Song by ..Ta-Ku Long time No see featuring Atu)

Control.. He Got Control Don't You Know
He has his Plan. He's The Master
Already been worked out in Ya Favor
God is on a Mission

23:48

Still up and its not midnight yet so I'm gonna keep it going. Don't want to miss out on a notion so why not pick up that pen & start the process. It's 11:44 and its still 7.8.19 and this was an entry I found that I just wrote on a random piece of paper and I just wanted to place it in a better location, so if you know how to be the world will be so EZ . What I'm saying is you learn how to pass over all the complaining and life becomes a breeze. So SIMPLE and FREE.. Over complicated rules never amazed me. SO BE FREE I gotta BE you know me, like the sun that shines so BRIGHT..IGNITE POWERS TO UNITE SO WE CAN BE..1LV...R.I.P SONIALEIMBERG

YESTERDAY

It's all gone, done and over but the memory is still here and it was a good day. It was my nephews 14ᵗʰ bday and all he wanted was some expensive iphone which he got and I still operate in the dinosaur era of android and just don't understand the children these days.

TRANSPARENCY

I love being straight forward I love being understood I love giving explanation. I do not like any form of miscommunication and it seems like I have this one person who gets me and that is not to say that others don't but it's been a long time since a man has understood me and I don't get to talk to him often but we do communicate. It's always a breath of fresh air and I really cannot tell you how great that is. Nothing like just being you and being open. I Love Life and I love being Open and I Love being good ol' Transparent Me 😊

BIRTHDAYS

We have them every year that we live, A celebration for the day with a cake and ice cream. So today was a celebration for my sister-n-law and she made 34 today and I made it just in time for a plate of tacos and a slice of cake. It was perfect timing for that sweet tooth craving and pray that she enjoyed her day like I enjoyed her cake. HAPPY BIRTHDAY!!

SELF - ACKNOWLEDGEMENT

Who loves you more? That is a question my mom would ask me when I was younger. Well once you reach a certain age in your life All of the affection and love that others gave you through your years that same amount of love & consideration you must learn to give that to self from self and constantly give back to self. You are very important to the flow of life and nobody will ever Love you MORE than You. NoBody, but GOD of course, but that's a given. So, everyday admire yourself, honor thyself for all of the good that you have given to others and acknowledge your worth and purpose and continue life. It Don't Stop Everyday you Live Stay Aware of Self and All That It's Worth Acknowledging.

PEACEFULNESS

Is there a more perfect scenery? I cannot think of any. Peacefulness is all I ask for. There are an array of scenarios that are awesome and perfect but please just keep civil and cool about it and I'm good. I Love a good vibing scene and I really am not fond of the boring ones but when that is the case I turn it into a sheer useful moment. Trust that, I need to be at peace at all times. And BOREDOM is not peaceful. You go crazy a lil' bit before you center self and find something productive to do. Anyhow, I'm in a very peaceful setting at this time. I'm in the backroom with my Gma and my youngest son while he has on headphones while watching a film on his PS4 I sit on this old shower chair and write this here piece while I sit in peace. I LOVE LIFE and soon I will be going into the kitchen to prepare dinner and then right into the peaceful evening I anticipate anyhow, cannot see it any other way and I have vision of this evening being calm so yes calm it will BE!! Until tomorrow which hopefully will be a very Peaceful Monday... HAPPY SUNDAY GN☺

TEMPTATION

Who wants to eat a whole pie? I would be a lie if I said I didn't, all creamy and full of filling. We all get tempted from time to time and crave for things that we know we shouldn't have but the soul wants what it wants when it wants it. Now not saying throw out the idea of control but what I am saying is that Well to be bluntly spoken, It just feels good sometimes. We are all non perfect human beings living a great experience, so, why not experience life to the max and live on the edge, just a little sometimes. As long as it won't do you, your body, or anybody else any harm, Go For IT and Indulge yourself in all of the things that make you say HMM!!

VISION

At the end of the rainbow At the end of a tunnel..The end goal. The final play has been made due to the way it was envisioned. If you are fortunate enough to visualize and accomplish what was set out in your vision that is great but somehow there are always interceptions that change up the game. STAY FOCUSED and KEEP those EYES OPEN! Although you can visualize with your eyes closed, having that capability of utilizing your eyes, what such a special sense that makes having a special eye for what is going on before you. I'm visualizing the bed now and about to take action and try it again tomorrow.

EXPECTATIONS

I don't have the answers to all things and I ask questions a lot. I like to have all facts to operate through my day. I try not to set my bar to high when I have to engage and or encounter others. And for the ones who I have shared some time with I don't give them a lot of failure space and I'm not sure if this is good or not but I Love them all without a doubt, so, whichever way the table turns and with the decisions that one makes we all just find a way to integrate how we are doing at that moment and get over all of what may be slightly less than anticipated but without a doubt we all get over ourselves, No Shade over here. I keep it real and don't have time for the junk. Don't set Expectations JUST BE AND LET BE!! 1LV

APPRECIATION

I Love and Appreciate all things. I believe to live a whole life with good and bad results derives from having the appreciation of all things. Even as crazy as it seems the not so pleasant events also can be turned into a positive outlook or learning lesson from the action that presented itself. However, live in the moment and genuinely pull from that and enjoy life and all that goes in and around in it. There is a lot to appreciate and give thanks for. Starting the day is the first gift of the day and then having mobility and good oxygen flow is the second gift of the day and there are a good flow of them after that. God has blessed my life and I truly have appreciated my life thus far for all that it has taught me. And to all of the lessons that we all go through share them and when the time is right and someone may appreciate your experience.

PREPAREDNESS

Priorities and Necessary are the two categories that keep all flowing accordingly. As long as you stay on top of the necessities there isn't a higher level of being prepared.

ACCEPTANCE

It is what it is, that's a real short and clear answer to a lot of things, especially to questions that you just can't seem to find an answer to at all. My new level of acceptance is my hair having a mind and energy of its very own. I have always understood hair is going to do whatever it wants but this is a whole new level. I am locking my hair or some call them dreads and they really aren't being very co operative. By being a women of such beautiful color I thought that my curls would for sure mind but, OH NO, not exactly, not exactly at all. So, my journey into not caring about my hair styles..I end up having to do my hair even more just to keep them twisted. They really do what they want and I have to learn to just go with the flow and really embrace all the ups and downs of this hair journey. My ankles are swollen right now and I never have time to rest even like now I'm sitting while my feet are dangling instead of propping them up. I have accepted that I'm getting older and need to rest every once in a while because these ankles look tired. OH MY, don't want to accept this one, so while I'm still going and can exercise I better accept that I NEED TO MAKE A MOVE and I ACCEPT THAT CHALLENGE. ACCEPTED 😄

CLOSURE

To put something to rest, the end, no more sleepless nights thinking about it. Today is Friday and I turned in some divorce paperwork today with a nice check along with it to be seen by the judge to rid myself of this terrible union. One that is antiquated and expired. And those papers signify that it's only a little while longer of a wait to the very end of this path, one that I could not do any longer, so therefore, I move on with the days and the movement in it. It feels good to put no good energy out with the trash. Centering self is important and with certain things put behind you it's easier to concentrate on self without the background noise or whatever needs some attention in some way. I just am crossing my fingers in my mind as I write this, that my case is pushed through and we can hurry up with the finalizing of our marriage story. To have complete closure.

ACCEPTANCE (RE -CAP)

I guess that is something that we must do daily. One way or another. Coming into full acknowledgement and acceptance are key components to daily living.

DEDICATION (WROTE WHILE SLEEPY)

Loyalty and Honesty are sure qualities needed to be dedicated to anything or anyone. Honesty Always and first on the list. And that means first with self. Staying true to the true self and then proceeding into grounds where dedication may come into the terms of the situation at hand and loyalty is not turning your back on the person or the project and that definitely defines dedication. I am dedicated to the One Almighty God YHWH, to my children, my life and my family. I am a person that feeds on vibrations and energy, so if there is ever a reason to question my loyalty I will definitely feel it and wonder why do you feel like that. I give my all in everything I do because that's all that I have, me my whole self and now I'm wondering where is this stemming from and the vibrations are changing now, I feel that there is a problem and for you to question my loyalty, what have you been up to? Now, I have to fill you out more and question if I should even go on through with you. Because that's just how it is, new friends are hard to make. Now projects, that's a totally different type of dedication.

REALIZATION

I have taken some time away from my favorite pastime activity. Realizing that life was moving and me not stopping for a second or two in my day to take action upon had me neglecting my hobby. Well, this is really more than a hobby, but the right words have not ran across my mind. So for now, Let the forces of the power BE what it is a hobby. I also have realized that my age really is nothing but a number R.I.P. AALIYAH, I surely do miss that artist. She would have come out with some sure hits if she were still alive. Realizing that those were the days with the good sounds to go with the times. I am also realizing that after a divorce and when you are completely over someone it is time to go and Enjoy Life Again. Not too Much Turn Down For What but EVERY ONCE AND A WHILE NEVER HURT ANYONE. Especially Moi, So, a new beginning is what I have come to realize the beautiful days ahead, What a beautiful realization!!

<u>R & R</u>

Those are the two letters my grandmother would always call out. And I never could understand why she called that out so often. Now, I know I need some R & R for sure, right about now in my life. For those who don't know much about these two letters they stand for Rest and Relaxation. Yes, those two letters are definitely needed in my life right about now. I am set to get a message by next weekend and I guess I will rest slightly, but I need more than an one hour nap. So, the rest part will be later in my life because that will require some days for me. I have been working since I could remember. Any kind of vacation will surely be nice, whenever that sweet day comes. So now my Gma is in her R & R days of life. I don't think this is what she envisioned R &R to look like though. It's alright though because she doesn't remember saying that phrase like once every other week.

ANALYZATION

At the end of it all or when it is all said and done you then have come to a conclusion & have analyzed the whole scenario and naturally, analyzations are made and I Love coming up with analyzations daily. That's all my mind does. Analyze Everyday.

COMFORT

Not to worry, Never to fear Everything is fine and self is sane. All that surrounds me is clear and calm. So the negative can be pushed away and removed as if it's as light as a feather. An at eased heart, rate stable and brain operating at its highest quality and ready to challenge the people in the day to just find their optimistic side and strive for that comfortable peace in their heart and to keep going with that same energy into the next day with that same goal of challenging the people to give their best in terms of social positivity. So we can all strive for a comfortable place to dwell in and it's called Earth. I am comfortable talking about all subjects and I'm comfortable being with only self. Although, I do like the comfort of being in the arms of a strong man who loves that same type of embracing companionship. Life has its not so comfortable moments and they definitely happen for reasons of course but when you are going through the rough matter that comfort level disappeared and wonder and confusion sets in and it's really never wanted, but, trust me, it's highly advised to just roll with the waves and work on your path to get back to state of comfort.

DYSFUNCTIONAL

Sometimes I am quite a bit dysfunctional, only due to the many responsibilities that I hold, attend to and that make me a lil' crazy by the end of the day, every once and a while. But, throughout it all I maintain my sanity, that use to be a rough thing for me in my years of being a newly wedded person. That man had to many expectations of me and that in itself is dysfunctional. As a human adult and at the age of 25 all expectations from others besides self should go out the door and just deal with what is given and or how things are answered in responding to what was asked of them. I have so much to do in less than three hours but I manage somehow to get all duties done yet and still and stand here and write just to fulfill my passion and to my mission also. Because I do believe in myself, so, I must always muster through all of my dysfunction and or Manage to just Function through it All.

ADVENTURE

My life is defined as an adventure, everyday is very different even when I do the same activity or duty or however. I like to make nothing but observations and analyzations. I love to trip on things around me and love even more to respond to things that interest me. I have three children and a granny, so, I have responsibilities everyday. This in itself is enough to write a book on but I will not expose them in that way. So, I'm 36 newly divorced and I'm stuck in limbo at the moment living at my mothers where I take care of my grandma. So, limbo may be a while, it just makes sense. Decisions that we make always lead us down a new path and sometimes the path isn't always what is wanted but in terms of need; most of the time that's the case. So my limbo life is alright because I don't need any privacy at the moment and I'm raising children and taking care of my granny so life is what it is and I take all of my limbo lifestyle and try to cherish these times for they won't be here forever. So, by today being the first of August lets see what kind of adventure the wild time of Leo has for me because trust Everyday is surely an Adventure..NJOY

INNOCENCE

I am not a child but still innocent, I believe in people, I believe in good nature and flow. I believe that God created us to live, thrive, and be as we wish in the midst of it all. Some would call that naïve but it's not what I would refer to it as, I have a really big heart, that maybe is too big and have to narrow my thinking a little bit but I am here to let you know that it's not possible today. I take my son to Del Taco to get a mini shake and I ask for a regular size instead and when I get to the window he said I don't know anyone was hip to the larger size. I told him well my children think out of the box and that is the way it should be. I don't look at anything in a normal way. I dissect everything and naturally want to know more just like a child, pure innocent, sweet as pie and don't really have any ill intentions unless I'm provoked to have such a totally different demeanor about myself. I must continue to keep my sweet innocent self away from the madness of the crazy world and pray for strength to persevere through the stages of life. I Have to keep my INNOCENT HEART

DEFINITION

As I sit and want to write more, I wanted to know the sure innocent meaning of Innocent and at the end of the sentence it said Ignorant. OH MY, Even though I can understand the word choice because they both do mean not being knowledgeable about a subject matter. I just shook my head and crunched my eyebrows inward or grimacing maybe a little because that was painful to read the word IGNORANT. What?? Anyways I will take my innocent reaction and keep my newly found knowledge put up so when I need it I can use my words accordingly. I love knowing the correct definition of words that I use, so, every once and a while look up a word and see the break down of synonyms. I am finally getting tired enough to go and lay it down now. A whole new day and its very full with duties that are there ready and I am pleased to say that things are all working well and that is defined by the powers of GOD so don't worry about things as such that's just me and my brain. My brain needs a definition ☺

DEVOTION

I am one devoted person. Over the years I have learned how important true devotion really is. First and foremost my love and true devotion to my LORD YHWH AND HIS SON YAHAWASHI. How I Love Them so Much or most people refer to them as God and Jesus. No, offense if you do, I feel they understand the struggle from living here on this planet with all of the false history to mislead the masses. Secondly, I am devoted to myself and my life which means that no matter how boring everyday life gets, I will stay true to myself & what I stand for which is peace and love amongst the masses which can be kind of difficult but with the correct amount of love directed in the correct way everything will be alright. Some days are very difficult to be right, speak right, and treat others right but I still try to stay devoted to my Lord and his wishes and treat one another with Love and Kindness... ReSpEcT Is Necessary!!

INTENTION

True intention is the best and with good backing the intention is even better, we all intend on great outcomes and great encounters but without the goodness none of these things will go great, so, being positive or a pinch of positivity will surely result into a great outcome. Today my intentions were to just relax with myself and God and that I am doing naturally, but my children won't let me fully get my dreamy day of peace. So, however, after all is said and done…Just be cool and have the positive vibe and you will go far.

FINDINGS

I have found my calling in my life it's to teach and to write, to reveal all of the ways that we can see an outcome from words and verbs played out to one another. Vibe with the day my name is CreChe and that rhymed, so, how you pronounce the name its so funky yet cool to be named after thee scenery that contains HE. NEED I SAY MORE..I WILL NEVER BORE NOR IGNORE. The way you or I feel that's the deal. I keep it way real, everyday cus that's the only way to be. Just flow with me you know I want to put it in a song and sing it out loud and just continue to BE ME FREE AND LOVELY and Lovely I'LL BE here in my happy space waiting until the day I see his face I'm glad I woke up today, I feel great and proud to BE ME, I am finding out more and more about ME everyday and Hey wait just a second I'm not conceded either I just like ME AND YOU TOO...UNTIL NEXT TIME ...JUST BE 😊

UNEXPECTED

My days are all filled with unexpected events throughout the day. Unexpected is the best way to experience life. A change of routine is always a good challenge for your life. Like a surprise party. So unexpected and what do you do? Enjoy the unexpected lovely energy that is directed toward you and even when the energy isn't so positive and the unexpectancies take you through the motions. I am in a state of single and my next love interest will totally be an unexpected gathering because I have no idea who will approach me but I have all of the time to be wined and dined to figure out who that special man will be. I'm praying a man that serves TMH and then serves me right loves me day and night and never puts up a fight. So, with all of that said I always put myself in sticky situations, now I must say I love to plot & play but in a good way. I just like to see the results from the other end because they are always unexpected.

SHOCKED

I had a boyfriend long ago, I got a job in his city to be oh so close to him. I stayed out at this house alot until one day when he stole from me and I was SHOCKED that's the least I can say but I got back what was taken from me eventually, by his little brother, after one random day when I decided to call. I am glad I did though, I got my Drivers License back and my wallet with no money in it of course, That's why he hid it when I was looking for it; going insane. We walked back to the store all searching in yards and in the house when he had it the whole time but however the case I once had a dream that we met again at a restaurant that happened to be his and it just made me stop and think about seeing him again in the future, thought for sure we would cross paths but not ever seeing him, so next best thing, social media FACEBOOK TO BE EXACT, I look for him and there are way too many people with that name and no photos stand out but today I type Long Beach behind his name and who popped up. So, I had to leave him a message just to clear the air on how I really feel. For a long time I have had him on my mind just to let him know I knew the truth and best wishes cus he just got married so WOW... WITHIN DIVINE TIMING..

DENIAL

Most people go into denial in desperate times. It is different for everyone and it comes in different ways for everyone. I currently have taken on some more responsibility. And here comes the denial when it comes to a parent that you have to start caring for, it puts you into the first stage of denial. Denial that she is getting weighed down with the meds from her illness. All while taking care of her mother whom is my GMA she seems to be in a slightly better condition than my mother and that definitely is hard to take in as a truth. More denial, then all while being the main person of care in the household I hold a lot of emotions which I hold together well until the denial which is just truth ignored settles in. So, there comes all the crazy energy that baffles me and overwhelms me from time to time all while being a mom to children who are also trying to take all the energy in around them as well.

DISTURBED

This date is troublesome to start off with because I will always associate this date which is the third of October with the day my dear old friend Gary Webb who is laying in rest. Now today I can write about him and think of him without getting upset or even get creeped out like when I was younger. He died very young, it was my 12th grade year. Wow, memories, well, next disturbance is my position at home. It is only disturbing because I am the only person who has to maintain all of the hardcore care and assistance for both of my family members. I am not bothered or annoyed by the amount of work, I am just sacrificing my sleep because I am needed all day and some of the night. So, naturally I get a little bent out of sort some days. But more so just like I wrote in my last message denial, it's really just hard some days accepting the truth of the matter. All while I understand and have accepted the truth, it hurts deep down inside. On many levels I try to justify but then always get broken back down to hard pinned up emotions that usually end up in tears. Lv 4 MOM.

3RD D - N -A- ROW

So, let us start it out with Daily!! Daily I pray for strength and patience with all my daily task challenges and any other encounters. Today I got a lil' bothered by all of my domesticated life duties that take over a large part of my day. I am not selfish so I do them without fuss, most days, until days like today. Lord thank you for my day and sorry if I offended my mother with my out loud cry of complaint about how there just isn't enough time in the day for all that I do, always leaving me blue because then All I can do is go to sleep no time for me. I love to write if I could I would, Although I am it isn't how I would like it to be. Just a lil' bit more often. So, I am going to run my day back right now from 6:20 a.m. when I woke up yesterday morning Sunday OCTOBER 6th 2019 to make my mom breakfast, help her get situated, go partake in a smoke break with a good friend, get a text asking to do some hair at 11:30, sit on the porch for 10 minutes in some sunlight, go check on mom, give granny a bath, make her breakfast and feed her, make my children some pancakes, then braid hair at 12:45 until 6:35. Finish cleaning clothes change moms bedding, go get some pizza to eat for dinner. Eat, go to the grocery store for lunch food and snacks. Wash more clothes. Change and feed my GMA, wash dishes, another load of clothes. Take my eldest son home with his dad. Pull up to drop him off. Talk to him for about 20 minutes. Drive back home to wash another load or 2 of clothes. Tell my mom GNITE adjust her pillows for her on the bed. Pull out my pen to sign some forms for a field trip. Pulled out my journal to use as a board to write on, and told myself I need to write in it, I got so frustrated today with all that. Yet, I must do it daily. Well I'm off again and its already Monday. I will write again tomorrow to compare the amount of work that I do in a day. I missed a few things in here but you can only imagine.

10.8.19 TOO TIRED= EXHAUSTED

It's October I'm 36 I have 3 children both parents and both grandmothers. I love Yahawah and I pray for the great opportunity to be in his grace. I pray I am entitled one day. Yahawashi died for all mankind and I love him too. As I listen to NATIVE AMERICAN flute pipe music. My soul moves to the heavens. I am so sleepy again, day started at 5:45 with my mom calling my phone so I could take her wet blanket off of her. Then back to bed for 20 minutes before I get to shower, then I go iron clothes make lunches, make mom breakfast. Drive children to school and from school back home. Then drive to Downey to finish up some paperwork then back home to make my gma some food, change her, feed her, then run back out to get these children something that they wanted from the dollar store, then back home to wash a load then pick my eldest son my nephew and their friend from school. Back home and really I'm too tired to remember at this moment. OHH WEE IM NO BUENO. 1LV CHE' GN.

HOW INTERESTING

As I begin to write I notice the date and I said HAHA so it happens to be my soon to be my ex husbands bday. I am in the middle of the proceedings of this agreement to go our own ways. However, the case I say unto thee It is a good nice vibe to the day. Birds are talking singing and the sun is blinging with light. I am tired still but I feel alright. My mother is coming along an old phrase that was said by many; many years ago. I pray that she won't be in much pain, that is the worst of all pain and then to witness someone endure is just as painful. That is my current story. I am balancing all of the energy around me and mine. I am multi-talented and fine like a glass of wine. Take that however you would like but guess what I'm gonna get it right! Right down to the point of energy. I felt it in me to go and grab this pen, it is my friend whenever my heart feels lonely, sad, mad, & even glad. I may just want to write, Express exactly how I'm feeling right at that time on a dime. I just pick up my friend and now I am sharing my energy like we are suppose to do. So guess what, Now its on you and I'm out. Deuces One Lv. Give Thanks to The Lord and you will feel alright.. Peace and Harmony as a collective. Unite. We can UNITE AND CONQUER THE UNIVERSE… POWER ALL DAY & NIGHT

SUCH LITTLE TIME

And not much room 2 write But I felt the need to ignite my pen to help me keep connected to my thoughts and to share never to despair in the moment, All is well and I know it. YHWH is All I want to know everyday I thank his Holy Name I pray that one day I will be fortunate enough to meet or bow down to the Throne. All I know is that time is upon time, sun til dusk, one day. 1LV …11.1.2019

SPIRIT

Spirit is always moving me, Spirit is always guiding me, Spirit keeping me free from the drama, Free from the madness that surrounds me. So many lies that have torn apart the lands. So many lies TMH has seen enough and has moved through some of his chosen people. Praying that many more will answer to the spirit. Put away all evil ways and try to come home with TMH, YHWH is his name. Live Love and BE under his Laws and ye may be saved. I Love my Lord I Love my Life because of him and I Love my Family and the whole nation that follows HIM. Destruction and Lies plague the land and the people in it. When he calls, you better answer, for if you don't, thy days are surely numbered to get it right. I pray for all to get it together. May YAHAWAH continue to work through all of us until we all unite for the greatness of HIS people and our Lord YHWH !! No name before his YHWH is King not Jesus, Praise and Blessings, Today is the day that the Lord has made, I will rejoice & BE GLAD in it…OOOOHHHH THIS IS THE DAY THAT THE LORD HAS MADE!! THE SABBATH IS TODAY.. KEEP THE LAWS!!

WAITING

I've been waiting here for a long time. I've been waiting for change I've been here anxiously waiting to see my great savior and I've been waiting for every good man and woman to speak of him. I've been waiting for the right energy and every good thing that follows. I've been waiting on the people to wake up and understand. I've been waiting a long time on you and me and we to come along and sing the same song HALLELUYAH for its Real . The God Of ISRAEL, The Holy Bible speaks of, the great book, there is no denying, he is waking up many. I'm a brown skin copper tone being. I Love who I am I sing in my cage until the door is let open and I sing loud because I can. I've been waiting for a true love to call my own, I've been waiting for all of the truths and understandings. The time is coming soon. The time I've been waiting for is now. The Time I've been waiting for is Now..YAHAWAH..1LV NOV 7 2019 11:07 FINISHED

TRUTHS

Are you and me

Truths

Will set you free

Truths

Are what keep people in the dark

Fighting against what just might be

Truths

Are you and me

Truths may be too shocking to bear

Truths can come up out from no where

Truths are an essence of beauty

Truths can make you some money

Truths go beyond your imagination

Truths can come up @ any occasion

Truths can take you far and wide

Truths are sometimes angled with pride

Truths are right under your nose, Literally

Pick up a book that is dated from way

Back in the past that's called History, And it will forever last

And That's the Truth!!

MAMAS

So right as I began to write this page my son came in to ask if he and His sister my niece and my play nephew/cousin could make a fort. So, he is waiting for an answer because they can't wait to get busy My niece is with me because my brother and sister -n-law are @ the hospital with my mama. She is feeling better than Thursday when she went in. So, they have to hold her this evening and since I have the three tonight my son was bored so I called my play aunt and asked is my nephew could spend the night. So, I went back to pick him up so all of the children could have a good time. I always have the children with me. I only have three children, but I always have owned vehicles that have three rows, why you ask.. Always have children with me!! So this day surely has been active, right before I got home I was with my granny for a few and before her, I was with my mama while she was getting some assistance from the pros at the hospital. It is crazy how now I'm the mama who always got mine and more to add to the bunch, we go a variety of places with different array of amounts but it always works out. My granny told me today that she had been thinking about me and she said Che on the tail end of her sentence, it made me smile ☺ She told me she loved me too. How I love being a mama who loves her mama and Big mama too and Aunt who is like a mama at times also. God Bless the Mamas!

NEVER ENDING

Amounts of love that is something that comes from above I can only say that I have been blessed enough to know and share the love because I care. I have three children four with taking care of my granny and five if you count my dog, but overall the love that I have is for all. Especially my kin, oh how I love thee. We are all so special to He. Although all don't know and are not aware, that's the thing that is not so rare. Not knowing how much love one has for you. We all think we know, but some will remain in a state of no concern I can say because I have a son who told his dad today that he doesn't want anything to do with me. I was also told this morning to learn in silence when all I was trying to do was pass on a little encouragement to the next sista who may be feeling blue, a little under the weather out of sorts but I get a rude comment that makes me say okay, I just need to step back and receive my love from the one and only He, because his love will never leave me or forsake thee because it's never ending and forever lasting. Lv me

A NEW DAY

Brings new outcomes and situations, my life is full of them. My children are healthy and well and my relationship with TMH YHWH is getting stronger each time I open my book and read for myself I learn so much and want to share and most of the time I do. It's apparent the time is now forgetting life and trying to align yourself with the highest power of them all. My life is full as I have mentioned and busy as usual when you have dependents the day runs into the night because it's just me to rely on to get it done. Luckily they are getting older and can atleast wash their own clothes but I stay in the kitchen because they eat breakfast and dinner so I am making 4 plates and sometimes 5 or 6 for the company that we keep and soon I will be a granny. More responsibilities, Although, not all lies on me but don't want to see the lil' one struggle at all you see. That's what grannies are for to make sure nobody falls, what a position to have but no need to fret because tomorrows a new day.

AWARE

Of the time

Will have you

On edge

Aware of your surroundings

Will make you

Pay attention more

Aware of today will make you ready

For tomorrow

Aware of the time means you understand

What all is here

Time is everything

And nothing is all in the same

Time is moving along and shifting energies

The Most High is Moving

To change the spectrum around us

Fast Warp Speed

So Stay

AWARE

PATIENCE

Is almost like having faith, faith is when you go for what you know and you put your trust in TMH God that all goes well and with patience you have to put all things aside and ask the most high God to help keep you calm during any given moment when you think you may not be able to do it by yourself. After an enormous amount of times of calling on the Lord above some may master the art of patience because they understand how TMH works and how he shows favor and mercy when you put your faith in him. But trust, patience runs low from time to time and that's okay. That means it's just time to go and have a talk with the creator because some things are starting to bother the core and that means that faith is also starting to run a little low. So, don't forget to stay patient with yourself and call on the man above to help restore that gift of patience within. Keep the faith and hold on my friend.

LONGING

For the day when I can see a great change. Longing for when the times will be free from chaos and pain. Longing for that time to come. Longing for us all to be one. Longing for the day when I get to see his face. Longing on the moment when I can say I'm free, today at last, freedom is here and I wish it was today but it's not so I must wait and long in my days of living, praying that we don't have much longer to go, each day is getting heavier and you can feel the pain. Longing to just get out of the hood where people are still stuck on Ignorance, petty and dumb things. I'm over it all and quite done, So, I'm longing everyday for a different page different life to begin A life without sin no where around me I cannot wait to be apart of that town. I will leave this all behind for that without a doubt because my whole life I've been longing.

SPIRITUAL

Powers are within us all, learning to use them is the highest challenge that presents itself here in our lives. A relationship with the Most High God is the first step to becoming spiritual. Once you have experienced some super natural or some out of this world type things occurs or maybe even a memory has you remembering how it was only an act of God could have pulled you out of the chaos and once you have come to realize that the powers over your life are really beyond our control. It is a wonderful experience to comprehend that our experience is spiritual. We are spirits that are using the body as a vessel to live here in the planet. I love TMH with all my heart and I pray that my spiritual powers only get greater. Be aware Praise the Lord always and Let the Spirit of YHWH move your spirit with gladness and greatness. I'm so grateful to know what I know SOUL2SOUL ONELV

PEARL

A rare true charm. Pearls are off white and are known for their beauty, I really don't see the beauty in them. Beauty is really in the eye of the beholder. I try to be that pearl when I am in a true valued relationship, for a true charm is what I am and it is up to my companion to see what pearl he has found. Pearl was also the word that I pointed to in the dictionary because I didn't have a word to write an entry on or about, pearls are worn by many just not by me I'd rather be one instead of adorning them.

SUGAR

I want some of your brown suga, I got that for ya when your ready, that's what I tell my man and that is the chorus of a song by D'Angelo and this will always be my favorite R&B Grown & Sexy first pick. Sugar is good and not good for you so watch your intake. It's never enough of the intake on the brown suga tip though Second random word pointed to in the dictionary. So, Sweet. Sugar!!

ECLIPSE #2

The full solar eclipse was 5 days ago now and I didn't get a chance to experience it yet again. Only visible in the southern hemisphere of the Americas. And in a few days on Monday the two planets Jupiter & Saturn will aligning at the same degree which will produce the Star of David or Star of Bethlehem, I forget the accurate term at this moment but it is something Biblical and I really do believe that this will have a huge impact on the world as if we aren't going through enough. Well in terms of letting go of people and things that don't serve me or my highest purpose, it's not hard to do, especially when there aren't many people in your circle to begin with. Since my last post on Eclipse clearing energy I spoke of a divorce and that was finalized March 2020 Thank YHWH up above for he treated everyone with disrespect. I have fell into a connection with a man I have known for about 20 years which is technically the longest amount of time I have known any man that I have even known or given the time of day to. I always thought I would never give in, but I finally did. Once I realized that the love that he has for me is real. It's unconditional, It's beyond patient because we still aren't a couple and it's a true friend that I have and that I have had for a very long time and that's the part that I love the most. I feel like we can just be who we are without trying to play a part to impress one another. So with me now in this connection I must continue to be patient and realize that true love isn't always perfect but its always right on time. So maybe I will catch the next eclipse and maybe we will watch it together. Who's to say what we will be by then but I pray he won't get put into the clearing eclipse energy.

FORGIVENESS

Is a gesture that is easy for some and very difficult for others. It also takes some time to contemplate and analyze the situation that occurred before you can come to the conclusion of forgiveness. It's always better to try to forgive and let it go. The more you hold on to the hurt betrayal or whatever had you in your feeling it just has you harboring that energy. Giving it energy Giving your energy to it. So, why, why waste your time and energy being upset about anything. My mother and father were two people in my life who I had to learn how to forgive. Now, I know a lot of people would question that statement, like how could I say these things and about parents that weren't abusive physically or anything. But my parents did things that I dealt with . It all happened for whatever reasons, and they did the things their way, I also learned to gain strength from unfortunate situations or unnecessary comments. I learned how to get through all of those things by telling myself it wasn't me and that they were only people trying to still figure out themselves, let alone being someones parent and so, I forgave them. It hurt but I learned what's behind the power of forgiveness... LOVE....

FOCUS

Is what I do to survive, every day is a walk in the park for me. Because I trust TMH with everything and most importantly my mind. He gives me the power to have control over myself, so I have mastered all thought processes and figured that the mind is the powerhouse, so, first and foremost I Thank the Lord for the strength and power of the mind then secondly keeping it strong. So, with that mind strong it has the ability to store everything properly. Everything in its proper category and or perfect order. Everything I do requires some sort of focus. Focus means you give it your time and or attention more like time and attention. Because everything takes time but not necessarily real focus and or attention. Like this entry is important to me because I'm midway done with my book of Random Life Entries so that's a Goal of Mine and That Requires my time and attention and that equates to Focus.

LOVE

Is a feeling that cannot be described, it's a verb that all should love to do. But, most of all its best when it's true. When it's real and genuine like the sun that comes out each day. Guaranteed to feel positive energy when it's real and if it's not real you will be able to feel it. Some confuse lust for love but lust is when you go on with your day. Love is when they don't leave your brain. Love is when you smile. Love is when you want to spend your time talking, laughing, and cuddling. More importantly, love is the key to true happiness and union between a man and woman together forever. Love will be the glue that holds it all together. True love never fades or ends. My love runs deep and it's like a flame that can never be put out. Powerful, hot, and ready to receive the same in return. Love is majestic. Love is Royal. Love is here for us all!!. Love TMH GOD LOVE YOURSELF AND BE OPEN TO LOVE 😊

ALIGNMENT POWER CREATION BREAKTHROUGH

WRITTEN 12.23.2020…2021 MANTRA

It's a Wednesday and this entry was titled based on a picture post I saw on Youtube and the picture showed one big word puzzle and it said on the top of the picture. (The first 4 words you find will be your mantra for 2021) Alignment is definitely a wonderful feeling, I am aligned properly divinely in my own power and with all of the great powerful energy that's gonna bring on this Breakthrough of Creation. It's time for the change, the time is now. The time is here and present and don't underestimate that you will have all the time to get things done with all this great energy. Just heard someone say be in your Aliveness. Yes, Life Force of the Aliveness and here for the Journey on all levels in life from people to experiences. Balance is key to all things and when you are completely balanced that's when you get the perfect Alignment with All Things 1LV BYE 2020

GRATEFUL

I am. Grateful is what moves me and moves through me continuously. For without the act of being grateful pride has an opportunity of taking over and then the ego starts to show and then you forget the process of how and who you are. I give thanks to TMH God 1st for allowing me to be transparent and capable of understanding why I need to be transparent. After overcoming all levels and learning how to control the flow of life and what it gives to you by being transparent, I can help someone gauge themselves and learn from seeing or asking how I did it. I'm so very grateful for the strength that I have been given to go the distance and strength to have patience. For in all that you do in a day patience is required, because without patience the day can become a bit hectic, and with the amount of duties to do with the amount of time we are given each day, it can get rough. And when you realize that time is never on your side you learn how to take it one day at a time and be Grateful in it.

CONSISTENCY

Is necessary for life to operate and flow with an even touch. I prefer to be consistent, even though sometimes God has other plans for my day and I may get thrown off course. I am alright with it because God gives me the endurance to get the job done regardless. I have children and dogs so I must be consistent, otherwise they pick up bad habits without even knowing. For they have no natural control or levels of discipline over their lives and or day to day lives. Although they are coming into the age of trying to figure it out it all and realizing all is work and they have to work at that. Consistency also requires balance because to be consistent you must manage your time to be able to put whatever you are trying to stay consistent with and put it into your schedule for the day. So, that's balancing time, and time has a mind of its own; so, you must be observant also too. To a certain degree anyhow, the list can go on and on about what all correlates and what it takes to be Consistent.

LIFE

Is within me and here it is as I pick up my pen. My son gives me this entry word tonight, the gift of life God has given to me. He picks this word which I have not written about not once yet, which was shocking when he said the word because when he gave me the answer after I asked him to give me a word. I even had the nerve to say Well let me look back to make sure I hadn't wrote an entry for this word LIFE…THANKS X:☺…Interjection… I have two puppies well one is almost one and one is one year old and the youngest life in a form of a dog is over here going crazy, he is jumping into the floors at his own shadow. No, seriously, he periodically does this. I say he is a little bit challenged with doing all that there. I pray he figures it out one day that it is just his shadow. Wow, anyhow back to the entry of Life, and yeah, No, I didn't have any entries in here with that title. Another word I figured I would have had in the beginning of this book of entries is the word Love. Wow, they both make good content. I could talk for days again just like I mentioned yesterday in the entry titled Consistency. I said that the list can go on and on about the correlations to that word so yeah on and on Life goes..

GOD

My niece gave me this word today and shocked once again, that I had not given honor, homage, praise and dedication unto the most important component to my life. God comes first in all things in my life. He has a name also God is just a little title that is universally used. God means power, YHWH IS HIS NAME, The Most High God of ISRAEL. Abraham, Isaac (Israel's Dad), and Jacob (whos name was changed to Israel). He has all the power and that's why I am shocked once again. I hadn't written ANYTHING yet. Well, there's never a day that I don't want to tell anyone about the goodness that he had done for me. He has a special plan and it's still being worked on daily and we are just merely characters in his story. I pray that I get to meet our great creator one day. I cannot wait until that day. Well, I pray I get to anyhow. He is so awesome and I cannot stress enough how awesome he is and how much mercy he shows to me each and every day. If you have never tried him, You gotta try him today. Call on him, He is Always Listening. Thank God for being able!!

ACCOMPLISH

Is to complete. I have accomplished so much in life. I can actually say that with confidence and proud to say that there are many more tasks in my future. I put my full energy and time into things that I take part in, so therefore it is accomplished with a smile on my face.... <(stopped here on 1.14.21).... >(started 2.23.21) There are many accomplishments that I have under my belt and I am grateful to be able to stand in my own power. Life is all about accomplishments, I am working toward accomplishing this book of entries also with two other projects that I am working on. I need to incorporate a better work schedule though and stick to it. I may be able to accomplish it faster. But when you're a procrastinator, accomplishments sometimes don't happen on time but they will. Well, I have accomplished my small goal for today. It was just to finish this entry that I started a whole month ago and now the next entry is a rude boy suggestion and I will accomplish that entry tonight too...(while typing this 4.29.22) I realized that the next entry that was written is a little to explicit and I want to inspire people not motivate perversions, so I KEPT IT OUT OF THIS BOOK☺

INSPIRATION

Comes from the root word inspire and to inspire means to uplift or encourage and a bit of motivation in there too. I chose this word next because I believe in the power of inspiration. Energy is real and good energy is a plus to be around. Usually inspirational people tend to be very high vibrational. Good energy people period can be inspiring. So, with that being said, my latest, my greatest inspirations are my children. I remember hearing that song before my first child was born and I played that song out. Beautiful song Google it Teddy Pendergrass is the artist. Very talented and as I write I promise to you I wasn't thinking about and or didn't have that song on my mind. That is just the way energy flows. I now too have just now inspired myself to do more than just an entry tonight but this weekend I'm writing my first Love Song because I'm a DREAMY KIND OF GAL.. SO, STAY INSPIRED..ONELOVE FULL MOON IN

VIRGO2NITE….2.27.2021

(4.29.22 AS I WRITE THIS, TOMORROW IS A NEW MOON IN TAURUS AND THE SABBATH..CANNOT WAIT) TOTALLY DREAMY…YOU TOO KEEP GOING..STAY INSPIRED!!

PERCEPTION

Is merely an idea or view of something. Like my perception of life is a bit much for some but those are my points of views. I perceive that this current energy that is radiating through the cosmos is just the change of energy we as a collective whole need for the sake of humanity, to be able to find that Golden Solution toward unity for all with sincerity attached to this mission. All that we do for our own selves and amongst others will move us in this new found direction that we are all embarking upon. Now even this new path that I am speaking upon once again is just a perception . Someone else may not feel that life has had any positivity attached to it lately with that dam Covid 19 running rampant and so many people scared out of their minds. These times are not for the weak. Only the strong will survive for sure and getting that Covid 19 vaXXXine shot because you believe it will keep you safe you have a different perception from me as to saying ONLY THE MOST HIGH GOD YHWH can Protect and Cover me not No Dam Shot. Do you really believe in the powers of the one and only TRUE GOD or not? I perceive that most don't but that's just my perception.

JUPITER

Is the planet that rules my zodiac sign which is Sagittarius, Jupiter is the largest planet in the universe. It's so large and blessings flowing overall, it's a great time. Being a Sag, life is pretty EZ going and some may call it luck. I just perceive it as good energy flow and being in sync with time. < (3.1.21 stopped) ...> (3.8.21 started) Now Jupiter got me on the 8th and I feel great in this place. My energy is on 8 because it's before 8a.m. I'm up early and feeling really great. So, I'm sure Jupiter has a play in that because like I said its 6:58a.m. the sun is coming out I'm messaging my feet listening to a video and doing this here entry to start my Monday morning. I also won $100 dollars a day after starting this entry. The card was only $5 dollars. I love when that happens. I just need the winnings to increase already!! For I have been playing for decades and It's Time for Jupiter to Release the Big Prize. Anything Big and Expansive Jupiter is behind that movement. So, when you hear about that great planet just know something great is coming in. Jupiter is my Ruling Planet and this Saggie is ready for Jupiter to do what it does best. Making things Abundant. That's Jupiter!!

TRANSITION

Into a new way of life or living. Transform into what you want and enjoy making the transition into the new. Moving forward in any situation is a form of transitioning. Don't Fear Change because with transition will be change. I am transitioning into a better woman daily. I am also transitioning my life into being connected to a beautiful soul. I cannot wait until we complete our transit into our new level of relationship, I feel that this is it. I don't want anyone else. HE'S MINE and I am enjoying this transition into our new level of life and love. There are many transitions of many kinds from positions at work to new love relationships. Transitions means growth in most cases, the only transition that does not come off as any positive change and that transition is the end of life. Depending on how you look at it, death is just a rebirth. So, is it as negative as we perceive it?

Transition yourself today in your thought process to see all the positivity in your life and let in all the positive energy. Transform your day, Enjoy your Transition!!

EMOTIONS

Are within all we do. From Happy to Down in the dumps. I can tend to control these feelings for the most part. Surprisingly, the other day I became a bit emotional and almost couldn't shake the feeling. Now, this sadness that came over me was with just due and perfect timing for I had never really had that kind of emotion arise in all of this time. My mom has been gone now for a year and 3 months and I was the strong force in the family and kept a smile through the whole process of losing my mother and keeping everyone else sane. So, I carried a large load on my own but with the Most High helping me. I handled it but to be able to have some old memories come to the surface and have the emotion of missing a loved one came over me. OH ME OH MY. A song named Keep Doing What Your Doing came on and got me going. Like she was happy with how I'm handled business here in my daily life. I am grateful for emotions and when you learn yourself and take the time to completely understand self , that's when you will be better at containing them. My emotions today are pretty even. Sun is out everyone is well Food Shelter Health Wealth Love and TMH ..EMOTIONALLY SOUND 3.9.21

BALANCE

Your life by doing a few simple things. First go to the Highest Power and repent, go and balance out your good and bad situations that have ran through your lifetime. After that process, all negativity should start to leave your presence especially the more you focus on positivity and wanting nothing more than to just have all things positive in your life. After mastering the balancing act of your life and who you are and how you want to be and or show up in the world everything becomes a lot easier in your world. I also emphasize your world because once you have mastered balancing your emotions, behaviors, responses, and mannerisms; you literally become a loner in the world. I say loner because there are not a lot of people who are truly balanced. And when your balanced you can spot an unbalanced person the minute they speak. All over the place these people hide in plain sight and most of them hide it inside. That is a depressed person usually. For sure that is a person who is unbalanced and hurt in one or many ways. One great opportunity that I have or any balanced person is being able to assist the unbalanced person by encouragement and great leadership. Leading them into a better direction and pathway of becoming BALANCED☺

HOT

Is the temperature when the sun is shining bright. I prefer the heat than the cold. My grandmother was listening to me while I was on the phone when I asked someone's suggestion for an entry word and she blurts out Hot. So, I said what did you say and she repeated the word. So, Hot it is. Make it Hot Mamas!! I'm only 38 and my grandchild will be here this month, and a lot of people have been telling me at least I will be a Hot and young one. I heard that 😊 Hot Granny in the building. I am actually hot at this moment with this heater on behind me. My vibe at this time is on high and that definitely is hot. Good energy equates to good strong flames of fire. I'm a fire sign so when my flame is ignited great things happen and when the flame is on low or no flame that's some cold energy. No sun No heat No energy. No bueno. I definitely need the heat to stay Hot 😊

CLARITY

Comes after you have taken out the time to collectively put all perspectives and any outcomes that matter to any given situation real thought. Real thought requires a lot of time and best if done in silence. Complete silence. The silence is so you can wrap your mind around all angles and perspectives and that takes real time. Clarity also can come in kind of easy. Easy in terms of much thought is not required because an action from someone may solidify the clarity that was needed for the final declaration on how you feel. Clarity just another word for conclusion. Once you have made a conclusion on something it has been wrapped up in your mind and you have clarity for the most part unless you have no real closure on what happened in a situation. Now, no closure is different, things must be talked out and emotions and scenarios of complaint must be discussed to come to an understanding or just a place of fair and conclude it with what you are left with, which still leads you to solidifying it. However, we do in our minds for Peace of Mind and Clarity

FASCINATING

How life moves as fast as it does. Time is precious. Time is endless. Time doesn't rewind and it moves rather fast. That is so fascinating to me. It has always taken my interest. I shall then say if it interest you it may be safe to say then it also fascinates you. I mean to a certain extent, I mean not all things that interest you but to be overly interested which is fascinated and it started with a small interest. So, my life is definitely a fascinating story and I am very interested in my own life and within my life at this moment I am taking interest in crystals and their healing properties. I also am interested in a great man that happens to be a great friend of mine. The way of explaining the fascination behind my interest in my friend is a real story. I began to take real interest on 9.11.2020 and that day was the very first day I really heard the question he had been asking me for over a decade and it's so fascinating to me how I finally saw him through different lenses. After that day our love for one another literally was activated and my love began to shift a bit in terms of how I loved him. I always loved him but Love him I had left that idea alone, but it came to the surface and I suppose that in itself was fascinating!

LIGHT

I am the light and I see and understand all that comes from the light. We all need to focus more on positive things and allow the light to shine through. The sun gives off light, the most powerful light ever. The Sun, illuminates, The Moon also gives off light. I mean how powerful that sun is. The sun gives energy to all living things. We all need that light to operate through our days. Being a light that shines bright like a diamond. Don't Stop Keep that Vibe, because the world needs it. We are all energetically connected whether we know it or not or if we want to be or not. It's just what it is. When you are filled with light and hold great powers the dark runs away with its tail between its legs. Scared little ones. Anyways know you have powers and they come from the light so you can go into the darkest of areas and never get lost because you know TMH God has your back because you have been trying to do right by him and by letting your light shine, so continue doing the work and Give The Light!!!

PROGRESSION

Comes from diligently working forward. Since we cannot go backwards in time something you cannot do., but degression; Oh yes, it is a thing. First off let us start with progression and that is positive movement. It means you are making the correct steps toward a particular goal or task. Great but when you take no steps or prolong out any action toward the goal is when you have now been put in the degression category. Procrastinators usually get a bad reputation but they actually get the job done. So that means that they do the work and progress. Progression equates to working toward completion and growth for some. Slackers have degression, slackers just don't do. Slackers talk a lot and have no action so they will 9 times out of 10 never progress. I am definitely progressing in my personal life. Writing in this book right now at this very moment is me being PROACTIVE knowing that I would like to be finish with these entries by summer so I can publish this here MASTERPIECE. Believe it and it shall BE. My mindset is strong never weak, that's a progressive mindset and with that being said my progression is at a good pace right now in my life. So, keep on pushing forward and Progress!!

ATMOSPHERE

Can be created or it can be natural, currently I am in an atmosphere that is comfortable. I am in a comfortable mood today. I didn't have any work today and had a wonderful evening with the man in my life. The atmosphere that I am in when I'm in his presence is blissful. I am so excited that my days are full of good vibes. I have been waiting for this my whole life. TMH God YHWH is so AWESOME he is a Master Planner because he set the atmosphere for me. I could not have planned this out if I thought I could. Timing is definitely Divine and so is this atmosphere. The atmosphere around you does have an affect on your mood, quiet opposed to noise, I don't like noise. So, a noisy atmosphere would make me a little irritated and a nice peaceful and quiet atmosphere keeps me nice, happy and calm. I also believe that it can be played visa versa, meaning that your mood can affect your atmosphere. So, peaceful atmosphere and here comes the loud noise. Now it's a different atmosphere. Energy and Atmosphere are one in the same. So, monitor your energy to create your Atmosphere

UNKNOWN

to mankind is the face of the creator. Nobody knows what he looks like. We have way too many angles and theories for anyone to know what's a sure thing or not. I feel like I am in one big unknown space. I want to know but I just can't seem to tap into the unknown, I am listening to a youtuber name I'd rather not say but he is always talking about people coming into the power of knowing what power each one of us have and some of the things that are about the universe and the unknown things attached to it. He now today is talking about how in our atmosphere plasma energy is coming down faster and faster. He also is talking about how the elite are leaving to Greenland and we have to redo it all and relearn how to do everything from farming to disposal of bodies. He said today is also the first day of 2013 not 2021 we have been using a different calendar that was made up. 2012 was suppose to be the end of the world according to the Mayan calendar. There was even a movie made about 2012 about the end of the earth. I still believe that the power of TMH is greater and I am not worried about what the elites are doing. They are in fear and they think that they have the upper hand on the outcomes of their future and what is coming to them from the powers of TMH because when he comes we they will for sure get a dose of the UNKNOWN!!!!

CONTENT

Means satisfied and or comfortable. I just heard my angel tell me write, write, write until your heart is content. I think that writing is the very best next thing to life itself. A form of communication that does a great service for some. Reading words instead of hearing is just a different feeling especially if you get an opportunity to see the actual handwriting. Penmanship is something that has been lost with time. Everyone is so content with the future of everything. People have literally forgotten how to spell and write in cursive. I may be content with writing and I use to only write when I wasn't feeling very lively in my life. Today there is a new moon energy in Aries and I am kind of off with my energy and need to release my emotions some way because I don't want to talk to anyone about it. I have always been able to get over my issues just with TMH GOD'S help alone. I am always content after talking to him, even if I still feel a little discontentment that may be lingering. I know it will be okay once I get over the disappointment that crossed my way. I believe my upsetness is a form of disappointment and this is another reason I love to write my brain picks up on my own energy and I answer some of my own issues and I must keep writing because I'm not content yet.

DISBELIEF

Takes me through a storm today because I went through a small one today. Well, like most days I arise from a nap not from a well rested nights rest. I still continue with my day with a positive mindset to get through all of my daily duties which are always obstacles to me because time is never in a slow movement its always moving so I must keep up with it and some of my task must be done in a timely manner. Like feeding my grandma or giving dogs medicine by a certain time. Getting my children up on time, all kind of things in a day and everyday differs. I feel like today I was being attacked spiritually, the past few days I have been in a very high vibrational energy and passing it onto all and any connections that past my way. I feel drained now after sharing all of my energy with the whole world and now I need to retract and regain all of my energy back. That requires me not talking and or interacting with anyone for a few days. I had a refrigerator that was delivered Saturday and today is Monday and there was water spraying from the back of the fridge so I go grab the hose and here comes water now spraying me in the face because it completely came apart. Huh What Okay, It took me three weeks to get a new fridge and now this I was so tired because it's a bit more to this story but I was in such disbelief that it was happening.........the saga continues...4.19.21

ANNOYED

Is definitely the mood that I am embodying at this moment even though I know I should be grateful and which I am always but I am still annoyed low key only because I understand and innerstand energy and how people and things surrounding you can affect your Inner G from time to time. I am glad that I got so annoyed because it pushed me over to my pen and pad to connect with you all. Whomever Reads This Far!! I have a small smile on my face now because I have slightly forgotten my dream which is to publish this by 2022. If I can by December that would be great too. Not impossible and me being so annoyed and with me now with my Dreams in Focus and Ready to Keep on with the Fight for Life, Positivity, Humanity, and Love for TMH. I must continue to write and I may just write all night just so you can see how my mind really goes and it will also be good for me tonight to PURGE MY ENERGY today and to put my thoughts into action so I can focus on my energy and change it and get out of this Annoyed State..... UHHH......4.19.21

MAGNIFICIENT

And worthy to be praised is his Holy Name. The Highest Power of the whole Universe. The Alpha and The Omega. The Beginning and The End. My one and only power, he is worthy for there is no explanation for not being in the mood for praising his name. Everyday is a new one with great opportunity attached and if you are into energy and knowing how it works in and out of your favor depending what energy field your in at the present time. I try to stay in a good vibe kind of energy all of the time so I can stay close to our highest source of greatness, but I am only a human that has great ordeal like type situations from time to time but overall it's in the right zone. I do need to take some time to refocus with my children, so they have a better understanding of their mother. I don't want to come across as non understanding but sometimes I don't want to hear the extras but today I stopped to ask a question about how they viewed all of the events that happened in one day that stopped me from getting to doing their hair and one child responded with yeah you were mad. Woah, What, Really so yeah The Most High is so Magnificent in how he knows just how to move us and now I know how to move because I am like my Father in Heaven Magnificiently Made because I Do GET IT!!

MARIJUANA

And I have an interesting connection. It was introduced to me back in the 80s. 1980's that is, Wow, Time...anyhow yeah All my folks smoked, I'm sure. For sure my dad, he is the main person who I knew of until I got older friends of mine who were smoking it .So, I began to see what the whole thing was about. Well, all I can say is that I found a friend in that green planet. I began a new frame of thought too. Overtime it became too much and it may had low key taken over my life. Fein like energy then had to check myself and slow up and then years into and stopping numerous times and starting over or back at it, sometimes I would question why am I spending this money on this? Well, I always spent money but then some years down the line fast forward to now in my life, I still feel like WTH , why should I spend all of this money on this one thing. Marijuana cost money now in these shops. So, it can get costly and that's crazy. It is just a vibe but realistically the vibe can be created without it, it's just we got so use to having it as a part of our lives, it's hard to shake and leave it alone. Once you start a thing with that green plant you are Forever in the Tribe of Marijuana...4.20.21

DECIPHER

Whether or not is usually how it goes. A decision that needs to be thought out first. Sometimes it involves comparison of things or just a simple choice between left and right. It's just a thought I now am going to the dictionary for a more concise meaning and then I will tell you the latest moment in my life where I had to decipher. Okay, and here we go, de- ci—pher (disi'fer) 1. to translate (a message in cipher or code) into ordinary understandable language; decode. 2. To make out the meaning of (ancient inscriptions, illegible writing, etc.) and also Google meaning says succeed in understanding, interpreting, or identifying something. But really guys I use the word quite often and its not to decode a message all the time necessarily. I know I spelled that wrong, however, The last thing I felt I had to decipher was negative energy around me and I had to weigh in on the people who were around me and feel out the energy that was around me and I had to decipher how I was feeling and how I wanted to proceed with each person after I was attacked with negative energy out of nowhere one thing after another. Really no, not really that's just energy and now I'm deciphering on how I feel about writing one more entry tonight. Let's see if you can decipher this one

DIRECTION

Speaks in multiple ways. Where and which way are you going and or moving is always the question. Some of us have an idea of the direction that we need to go in. At this current time in my life the direction I'm moving in is forward. I don't do backwards, that is not a good way to go and or focus on. Always move forward. 333 mind body and spirit gotta keep moving. I am continuing moving forward like the publishing of this book that I am always working on. I know with all of my heart that positive efforts produce positive results. It has almost been two years in the making and working toward my goals. I get tired with all of my daily duties and responsibilities but I'm forever motivated to follow through with all of my good energy that I need to express upon to many and pray that with all of my good intention the direction of any energy around me can and will help change ones vibe for the better. So that means I just need to be me, Always, moving in a forward direction and being a light. Light for anyone to follow. All I want is to continue going in the right direction and assist others to move in the Right Direction too...4.26.21

PERSISTED

On through my hurt and still came out on top. If you don't go within and reach for your strength you may not make it through a situation that needs some extra attention. Not every task or duty comes with ease. Complications do arise and with that being said I have had many trails in my life where I had to lean on my inner strength which is TMH God to help guide me through step by step. Strategizing my moves, Diligently moving in the flow of each day. For I am aligned with the understanding that I am not in control of time and the things that can alter a situation at any given moment and when things like that occur oh wow how things happen and throw monkey wrenches in your pathway. Monkey wrench means a challenge, a nail in your tire energy while trying to achieve something already planned. Staying calm is the first key component and key to being persistent and being able to follow through to the completion of a task. After many decades of living, falling, trying, succeeding, to falling again I never gave up on my life. I also have many people who I live for, my life exist of great people and relationships, that's what I live for. So, through all of my adversities, I never saw it being the end so I persisted to proceed to find the Light. 4.26.21

ENERGY #2

(Scorpio Full Moon Tonight)

Energy is ME. Energy is YOU and now there is two I just felt like rhyming and did you know that everything is done in divine timing. As I speak to you through this pen I must say its all in the feel of everything. It all just keeps me going, flowing, feeling good energetically, at my highest peak, sitting on a couch, but I see myself looking over the ledge, at the top of the land, where I can see everything so clear, and all is there for me to be. To be free. To be me. Able to soar as high as I'd like, that's my energy. Always and ready for just about anything. My energy is kind of hard to match to a T. but I am not one that will make you feel low or less than. I'm gonna give you a small lil' lesson to catch up to me and its only a small dose of me because too much of this energy and you may explode and or just shut down and begin to mold. And since I live to spread Love I take my time I use my mind and try to connect to everyone one step at a time. Love Rules and God is Love He gives me nothing but his Love and for that I AM FOREVER SO GRATEFUL YHWH IS MY LIFE AND I KNOW WHO HE IS TO ME AND WHO HE MADE ME TO BE!!! I have broken free from society to be me a God FEARING WOMAN WHO LISTENED TO MY ENERGY!!!

RECEPTIVE

(SUPER PINK MOON)

I will forever be. It's 555 on my clock right at this moment. Numerology is alive and well. TMH is here Always and Forever, I receive all of what he will allow in my life. 555 represents change and that is a definite fact. Today is April 26th 2021, and I am listening to a reader and she is such a good reader. The title of her video is Devil vs God : Choices dependent on your Future. I'm still a little baffled by the title but I believe she is just saying The Future is and will be affected by choices. I guess her word choice just doesn't settle well but however, that's not important. It's just what she was talking about as I'm writing about TMH, Numerology and listening to a reading. Those three things together are seen as Taboo, forbidden, or out of alignment according to some religious people. However, I also am receptive to the ideology of religion of any category. The best Love that one can be receptive to comes from the TMH GOD YHWH and that will be the best Foundation to move upon and all the strength that is needed to proceed in a forward direction toward success with all things in ones life. Being open to new ideas and new beginnings and just ready to take a leap of faith into anything is also just like being receptive. LET GO & LET GOD 4.26.21

TRIBAL

Code YHWH is the only tribe I need to claim. Once one decides to be apart of his tribe life changes forever. Focus and detail is required in all that you involve yourself in and or with. Staying dedicated to the tribe is what will change the world for the better. He is the main leader and then there are sub tribes underneath him. Within each tribe the rules of the main tribal leader has set aside for all to follow. One main rule to follow is to give TMH praise for keeping you upright then staying in a positive outlook on life type of attitude toward life and trails may arise but with him truly by your side it's just a lesson. I have a tribe of my own me and my three and I must focus on making sure they understand their role in life as a child of God and what being apart of this tribe really means. This world is full of temptations but when you are constantly in search of trying to overcome all distractions and what that truly means, it will put you into a place of knowing how strong and wise you are. Coming into contact with all things that are in your surroundings good and bad and being able to overcome all temptations and distractions of the world is when you realize it's really a TRIBAL THING 1 LOVE YHWH.

GLORIFY

His holy name. It's YHWH, do you know him? I pray for mankind every-day and extend my heart out with positive energy and thoughts in prayer that those who don't know him will hurry up before it's too late. I have heard that the time is up, but I am not TMH and neither are the people who have said that. So, how can I relay a message that I have no real answer to. Individuality is important because we all are our own entities and all have our own personal lives and within our lives each individual person is responsible for their own personal search for the truth. Within finding that truth you should find the POWERS THAT BE OVER ALL. YHWH is his name the holy father above who created ALL. I can only think of one who is worthy of being glorified. That's just how I see things. My grandmother and some have the name with the root word Glory in it. How nice the name is and sounds but Glory means a great honor and admiration won by doing something important or valuable; fame; renown worshipful adoration or praise. Heaven or the bliss of heaven, a halo a circle of light. To be very proud rejoice and exalt and YHWH is the ONLY GLORIOUS ONE FOR ME, AND IS WORTHY OF GLORIFYING.

ALIGNMENT

With anything you are involved with should always be the case. I need to be aligned with everything I do because if I'm not in alignment that more than likely means the energy is not matched well. Matching energy amongst people is always important because it's better to work with those type of people who are kind of like yourself. Naturally I cannot leave out how the highest of highest relationship with TMH GOD is the first in line when it comes to me and my alignment. I knew in order for me to know TMH I would have to align myself when doing tasks and even within my thought process and staying focused on doing the right thing and saying the correct things. Basically, saying the foundation should be positive and with good intentions. That's why the saying goes like this, "change starts with self and one day one person at a time" Once you have aligned self to the best which is TMH and are being an example of well roundedness, positivity and Love for TMH, people will see how TMH protects and provides. So, one person at a time is fine by me. I just pray that I will help many especially those who want more for their lives. My life is constantly changing but I have no fear because I let GO AND LET GOD many moons ago. My Mind Body and Soul will forever stay in ALIGNMENT WITH YHWH 4.28.21

DECISIONS

Are made all throughout the day. It is Thursday start of the day and I have made my first decision of my day to write. I didn't write that much yesterday, so, here I am writing a small message to you while I am listening to a video and she is such a good reader. I always make the concrete decision of watching and or listening to her specific videos. You may wonder why and I can just tell you this, I appreciate her physic abilities and right now in her video there is a lot of para normal activity like her Alexa going off asking her what should she take note of? The response she gave was okay, I wasn't ready for that, but she brushes it off like it is just a sign. Maybe someone needs to take notes while she speaks. I took it as that as well, but she must remember also that it is technology. Technology has intelligence and each device has its own mind. Each device decides to move independently from time to time just like her reading today is completely different from any other style she usually does. So, for whatever reason her decision to do such still aligns with my title. I will continue with this video as I write my next entry because that's my decision and by listening to her I hear a lot of good information and to some she may come off as fake and they think she is creating illusions for people. As she just said the word literally "disillusioned" THAT PART!! Make Wise Decisions Always..

ILLUSIONS

Are just mere subconscious thoughts, definition in dictionary, a false idea or conception, unreal, deceptive or misleading appearance or image. Hallucination or a false impression. I am far from false so I guess that's why I don't deal with illusions. I have been fooled many times by the illusions that were all around me. Life can seem as an illusion some days with how well a day can go. I pray that my feelings at this moment toward a special person is not an illusion. As she just said again as I'm writing time is an illusion!!! I'm done with her today and that is why I watch her and decided to continue writing while listening. Our energies are aligned big time and I get clarity every time I listen to her. It could be anything, like her message is talking about a special woman who knows a lot taking a bath in her card that she sees. I was just telling my children yesterday I will be staying at a hotel in a few days so I can go and take a bath. I have a bath in my home but I wash my dogs in that bath. So,my thoughts movements and decisions within my day are clear and all things start as a thought and most of my thoughts are clear and I can see them in my mind like photos or visions and in my younger years I sometimes would question my visions and viewed them as ILLUSIONS.

ILLUMINATE

All situations by bringing light to the situation and who is illuminating situations at this moment. The women who I'm listening to she brings awareness to certain situations. She brings her gift to the world and some will reject her gift of light and how she harnesses her energy. Light is a form of energy. If you are reading this more than likely your energy is of the light as well, also we are known as light beings. I love being the light, I love bringing my light to all situations on all levels and now I have to pause right here because I need to go and be the light for my grandmother who is bedridden and go and feed her and talk to her which is enlightening in a way where I just am bringing light energy to her and illuminating her space. All a form of illumination, It's no coincidence that when I decide to pick up and write really quickly that it would lead me to an entry that was half done. So where do I pick up the conversation after I said it's no coincidence and with saying that I am now getting ready to go and clean up my granny again and I told myself go write one really quick. So funny because my duties never stop. By always doing so much work for others and even myself my light is shining all the time. Work with mad efforts attached with great intentions of allowing the light to Illuminate the whole world I'm just busy indoors right now but my light is still shining just with my loved ones. So, they all can continue to live off the illumination that I bring to them.

INVESTIGATE

All things that come into your life. When I say trust nothing or nobody that is the truth. I investigate daily. Sometimes without any effort put into any of these investigations, proof always arises on its own. Not saying I'm living around a bunch of liars. Well, not in my corner anyhow. I do a lot of research online and have done quite a bit of investigating about all the lies that the whole world has inherited. Many many stories and theories apart of this whole big lie that is set up and around the world. Starting with Government being the first organization to house all lies and then they take the truth and manipulate it and twist it upside down. I am going to be really honest right now. Okay I'm investigating right now at this very moment. I am listening to a read right now and all of the ones I have been watching for the past two weeks have been in the same energy zone. Karmic exes causing mad issues, being jealous and spiteful. I understand that the road can be rocky due to the relationship just ending. It's fresh even though he tells me they have no connection and every weekend since we started talking I have seen him and we talked everyday. Energy is vibing high but the past few days our energy level died down just a bit. Now this is great for reflection so when we take out time for reflection I also have time to investigate..

INTERPRET

My words, interpret my mind, interpret my heart now what did you find? Within this book of entries I have given you many interpretations of how and what I see, think feel and or understand. The brain is the most magnificent instrument known to man. I utilize mine everyday constantly, I love interacting with others because my mind loves to collect analyze and dissect. I find people to be ever so interesting. We come in so many variants it's ridiculous but radically cool. We all interpret things differently too that's what makes interaction with others cool. Perspectives always make any situation worthwhile. Just like at the top of this page I wrote some small notations about some things my favorite speaker was speaking on and spirit takes over when I listen to her because somethings I can really relate to and or she will say something that I spoke about a day ago or something wacky like that. Analyzing and being able to interpret it and apply it to self is what I do a lot when I listen to others. It's all about how you receive it because believe me there is such a thing as to be misinterpreted. Good Lord. I don't like any form of MIS.. So, lets just take it one day at a time and one situation at a time so all can be interpreted properly

CHEMISTRY

Known for the mixing up of formulas for experiments in science also in the human nature between two. Chemistry between two people apply the same, it still comes with variables, formulas for experiments and of course results. When two variables mix well we call this good chemistry. After the chemistry is detected then extra additives are added to see if the results change or stay the same. I have been a variable for many years and have been in many equations or experiments. Also many experiments with good results just not too good with the additives added then the outcome ends up changing and the results are extreme and experiment is over. Shortly after a new experiment would be started up again or on the To Do List. Fortunately, at this current time in my life I am apart of an equation with a variable with exponents and although we have had an additive or two our results didn't change so that kind of chemistry is great. Great variables Great equations Great experiments Great results. It doesn't get any better than this, now just for the record I never took the subject in High School but I know they whip up some concoctions in that class the subject of Chemistry.

CONSCIOUSNESS

Is to be aware of what is going on around you. Being mindful of your environment is being conscious. In my conscious mind at this moment I am completely aware of what's going on. Right now at this time in my life. I have so many daily duties so I must stay conscious of what I'm doing along with time. So, as I sit here writing in this book while sitting with my feet in the foot massager, I know I cannot sit here too long because I have many other things to do. I also am listening to a reader. Something I love to do especially while writing because of some linkage in communications and meshing of energies is what does it for me and so she is talking about how much the other party in my love life is thinking about me heavily but in fear of having that talk so, subconsciously and consciously I am always thinking about our status and where it's going. As I focus on my future and the publication of this book within my day I am consciously thinking I need to go take a small break because I am consciously aware that this is the time for action. Action is required. Action is the key word in her last sentence before she ended her reading as I'm coming up on my ending, even up to the amount of space requires consciousness!! (written in a normal composition book before typed)

COMPASSION

Comes from your heart space, having compassion is one of thee greatest forms of love. Love is great and has many levels but the fundamental part of it all everything has a foundation. A bases and love even has a foundation. Compassion is the base so how do you define compassion CreChe? Hmmm. Thoughtfulness while caring and or being gentle. Showing love is so important to me, not only am I one of those I love Love type of folks but seriously I believe that genuine Love from the heart can be felt so to pass on the High Love Vibrations to keep it going pay it forward daily. Knowing that you have sown good product is usually what we reap. Positive equals positive. Compassion can change the world. Love may be too heavy of a word to use on a daily with folks, you don't know but really it's all good. If you feel it, you may lift someone's spirit. Some people are never told that they are loved. That's so sad, Hey, Look Here I got soooooo much compassion deep down in my heart I just want to tell you , I LOVE YOU AND ALWAYS SHOW COMPASSION

COMPONENT

To component simple terms part to part. We use words like component for multiple different nouns. Anything can be a component you yourself can be called a component lets continue with this connectivity with this word component and this book. Once again I'm watching a video or listening to a video with one of my favorite readers. Victoria is a component in my life right now for sure. Right now she is talking about the energy she is picking up on which she channeled,the High PRIESTESS, which represents the intuition and I use my intuition for my whole life. That is a major component of my lifestyle, my mindset, and process. All altered by my intuition. So, components are literally whatever you want a component to be, my pen, this book, my phone all things are components. When equipment breaks down new components. When equipment breaks down new components will be needed to fix the issue. This word is pretty straight forward, I suppose because my brain didn't just flow with speed while gaging my space to create . So, lets see what the dictonary says to complete this page so, it says to compose, serving as one of the parts of a whole & an element or ingredient. So, like I said, component can be anything you want a component to be..Thank you for reading this component ONELV..5.11.21

GOD #2

Is forever the highest of powers. Powers beyond ones imagination. I am unaware as to why some are atheist. I will never understand it. I am not even saying full Bible believer or anything I mean just even on a spiritual tip, no I mean they just don't believe. I mean I don't know how I could bypass the fact that I did not create the human or anything around but I guess that's just my way of thinking. You know I am just curious what the dictionary says and this time it's not just to fill in space, but I truly am curious. It says to call out to, invoke, any of various beings conceived of as supernatural, immortal, and having special powers over the lives and affairs of people and the course of nature; deity, a male deity, an image that is worshipped. I mean all the way at the end it says CREATOR. And ruler of the Universe, regarded as eternal, infinite ALMIGHTY. Yes, Yes, HE IS ALMIGHTY and very worthy of being praised. If you happen to be in question of who God is I pray you get to know him. He is so great and is always with you. There is never a dull moment when you rely on him for all backing throughout the day. IF it would not had been for the Love of TMH GOD YHWH I really don't know where I would be.. GOD IS SO GOOD, GOD IS EVERYTHING!!! APTTMH..ALL PRAISES TO THE MOST HIGH YHWH..ONELV

GENESIS

Is the beginning of it. The first book in the Bible and now let's start the entry with the real definition and it states Birth, generation, to be born, the way in which something comes to be; beginning, origin and finally it states the first book of the BIBLE, giving an account of the creation of the universe, with all of that said yes, a new start, Roots, Beginnings of Life and Time as we as mankind know of. All of mankind should want to take their understandings of all things to the state of Genesis. The origin as I pick up my pen again to continue on my journey that began almost 2 years ago now. That makes me really proud to say, wow, the growth that has taken place within that time I even had began to read the Bible and the first book in the book is really quite interesting. You will find out more than you think. The origin of mankind or at least that's what we've been told. I will always lean toward the ideology and believe that. We are suppose to try to live accordingly , actually more Christ like, just a thought a small thought. I know I am no where near perfect and this life is a whole maze but best believe when you do believe in the Creator of Mankind you believe in the HOLY BOOK that's the greatest book known to the whole world and it starts with the book Genesis.

GRANDPARENTS

Are so sweet, you are suppose to have four to start off with, if you are blessed maybe more. However, and whichever way it happens to be and how many you get to call and or greet with hugs and kisses they are the best and there is no denying that. Well, let me speak for myself I was wealthy and not financially but in Love; growing up I had all four. Power Houses they all were individually, so I had a lot of personality to grow and learn from. They also were the best because they always were on my side when my parents thought I needed to be punished, but don't it twisted though, they can flip the switch too if need be, I even remember once my grandpa telling my brother I'm going outside to go get a switch. I even knew that there was nothing good with that statement because for one I had never heard of anything like that, so yeah, you gotta give the grandparents mad respect because they lived through parenthood.(I'm laughing) and then excited to be parents again, in the second half of their lives when life should be child free beach going everyday kind of living but I guess for some grandparents like mine they could if they wanted to but they knew that we could be returned to our parents. But grandmas like mom was (R.I.P Mom) she didn't have that choice because I lived with her with my first second and third child. What would we do without the worlds greatest people Grandparents…5.11.21

<u>LOVE #2</u>

can really change the overall foundation of any situation. Love is powerful. Love can make the sun come out. Love is a smile. Love is wonderful and sweet.. It's makes you feel complete without it it's a lonely place to be or feeling to experience. I'm smiling right now because I'm loving someone and he doesn't even know it. He makes me smile and I never regret my time spent with him. Relationships at this stage in my life is surely interesting but luckily I'm not knee deep in my ages but approaching, I'm just saying. Life is different when you are a parent and not getting parent approval to do and or be. Life is different just a lil' bit when you fall in love for the 2nd time around. It may blow your mind. Simply because you may of thought of giving up on that thing called Love. Didn't ever think that something like that is possible. Well, it is at any age, giving someone else your time and attention, someone new is always good. The thought even runs across your mind could this be true and yeah I think it really is. I think it really could be Love looking at me once again with a smile. That is always on my face when I think of him or send a text and please don't let him call. I'm gonna be ready for whatever he has planned. Love will make you giddy and ready for whatever and ready to flow like the wind. Love is beautiful my friend and I pray you find Love or have someone in your life who you can call your tru Love.

LOGIC

Requires what?? Thought. Usage of your brain. Organization. Without logic that is when chaos starts. No order, no control over the situation equates to being illogical. Interesting on the point that my mother my grandmother and my sister n law all worked for Logistic companies. Transportation companies that keep up with peoples merchandise, time, truckers, all cities, all codes and yeah, so, logic is required for this job. I would always turn down the option to learn the secret code language of logistics or transportation. My mom would always try to get me to learn so I could get a job doing the same thing as her. Unsuccessful she was but she was successful with my sister in law. She sure was, however, the case there is also a rapper with the name logic. I am not sure if I like his music or not, I am using so much logic at this moment. While my main focus is to finish writing this book I must use my time wisely. So, I chronologically move to make sure I get all of my duties done in a day. So, currently I have my feet in my foot massager while writing, That's Logic!! Killing two birds with one stone. That's an old saying and once I am done with this I have clothes and dishes to wash and floors to wipe down and lastly clean and feed my granny. Let's not talk about logic, my brain is always on and even when I'M SLEEP , I'M USING LOGIC!!

VARIABLE

Or a variety of components. That is how I see it. In math equations the letters are known as a variable so therefore it can be a variety of things that can represent the word variable. I am a variable in many equations. I have many family members, many friends, and many pets and they all are a form of relation to me. So, with each relationship I am a variable in each one of those equations. I value all of the relationships that I have and I have never thought about just how many equations I am apart of. Math is still one of my favorite subjects. Math really opens the mind and the brain also it expands in size, the heavier the math gets. I do have the desire to return to school I just haven't got the time to dedicate to those types of studies at this time in my life. The day goes so fast it's insane and it makes me feel quite crazy, I'm telling you because I'm in so many equations waiting to be solved each day and all day. I'm quite busy that's all I'm saying and some problems take longer to solve than others, but that's just the way it goes. There are levels to it. Easy, slightly challenging, difficult, and extremely complicated. Interesting how you really can explain life in a mathematical type of way and how math helps with the expansion of the brain and the mind is just another Variable!

PREVAIL

Over all that comes your way. Prevail because you can. Prevail for you. Prevail for your future. Prevail for tomorrow and forever. Prevail in the face of fear and the unknown. Prevail when they said OH SHUT UP AND GO HOME. Prevail all the way to the throne. Prevail all the way for the Kingdom. Prevail because its not all bad. Prevail for you know nothing better. Prevail and never say never. Prevail and never be a taker be a provider a rider and let the people know how to prevail, you gotta trail down a certain road some may go astray but all you gotta do is continue to try to stay in has grace. Not too difficult focus on self first and trying to do it right. Learning how to start at ground zero and prevailing and conquering through the steps while stepping to a different beat but when it runs through your soul you can't wait to integrate, exchange and influence the next being that could end up saving someone and by helping another person here in this place is my mission. So, I must prevail I must continue to dance to my beat and roll with TMH he is my music he helps me with my whole existence. So, with this pen and my mind and my energy flowing through to this paper I have prevailed once again with a small message and it was on how to prevail..5.13.21

PURGE

Let go and Let God is one of my favorite sayings. To Purge literally means let go throw out destroy all things of no value. Now I must see the actual meaning and it says to cleanse or rid of impurities, foreign matter or undesirable elements to cleanse of guilt, sin or ceremonial defilement. Even to empty bowels. HAHA. OHKAY! Well, I know you didn't ask for the last one but I figure Ahh what they hey. Just a little emptying my potty mind if you will. Ohkay I know I will keep my day job and write only and stay away from the comedy sector. I need to purge and drink water only and eat veggies only for this fast food world is killing me slowly. So, as I write this sentence I am coming back to this entry on a whole different day with new energy and let me tell you how I purged today after a moment of being in my gluten mode and ordered two banana splits from Baskin Robins today and couldn't even finish one. I ended up giving the other one to my eldest son…THANKS JA… because I didn't even want to see it sitting in the freezer. That banana split will cause a for sure purging of my system. I'm just saying, I keep it real and straight up all the time! I appreciate whomever you are reading this I am forever Grateful for you and I want you to find time to relax surrender and purge to restart.

EMBRACE

Each moment of the day. For every moment is different from the last. As soon as I picked up my pen my cousin June Bug called. I want to write so badly but I cherish my family time and considering that he lives in Texas I never get to see him so I stopped writing to embrace that time spent on the phone with my kin folk and give that call my attention. That also happened earlier too. I was getting ready to go and clean up my backyard but my phone rang and stopped my progress. If it wasn't my dad calling I for sure would have continued on my path of cleaning. I definitely embrace all of those seconds when I speak with him for he too doesn't live near and I only have him left and therefore I appreciate and value our relationship and being able to have moments that I can embrace myself upon and take those moments and have them forever in my heart because I do cherish them. And for the last comment for this topic is when you have the opportunity to be in love with someone and being able to be in each others EMBRACE.....Priceless!!

RE- EVALUATE

Your thoughts from time to time. Re- Evaluate your process from time to time. Re- Evaluate self from time to time. I must constantly re- evaluate my daily schedule and the time that I'm given in a day. It's 11:23 p.m. on a Thursday evening in May of 2021 and I wanted to release while listening to this Jazzy piece, I just wanted to vibrate by singing and writing. The man I am involved with has me in my feelings and he still doesn't have a clue and it's puzzling me as to if I should re evaluate how I approach the situation. I'm trying to be low key because he is not showing any real emotions besides the fact that the relations between each other are extreme flames that have that your mine like feel to our relationship because I have known him for 20 years. So, I can find myself deep in my feelings or emotions about him, I am also trying to consider how he may be feeling coming out of a long ass relationship that was full of drama. So, I don't want to be just a rebound or someone he just gets his high for the week and off to the work week, children and work for us both. So, just when things move in such a slow manner, I am not use to that, I have to take a step back and RE- EVALUATE..1132 P.M.

PRACTICAL

Kind of day is what I can say about today. It's Friday and I start my day thanking TMH GOD YHWH for my day and then I watch a video or two about the current energies of the day and maybe one to two current scenarios circulating in the world. I also light a candle or two also just to have a pleasant smell taking over the home. I then take my attention to my children and wake them up for school and make breakfast for them. Grandma is up next for my time she needs to be cleansed & fed then I can take a shower and relax for a bit. So, it's now that time that I would go and take my shower but I sat down to write because I am so excited about coming up to a completion of this project. I have such a practical way of thought also, So, last night I was quoted a price to publish 200 books and it was a little outrageous I thought when I first saw the price pop up but in all actuality the price is correct and right on the money so on the money it makes perfect sense and very practical in price considering the work they do for you. When I sale the book I will sale it for 24.44 and I should receive more than breaking even. I will continue to put my good vibes into the world so, I know that won't be difficult, see I even think in a way that is so Practical...5.14.21. 4:44p.m.

RESULTS

Are going to be great. You just wait and see. The world is yours and mine. So, lets take over and be great together. There are enough fortunate outcomes for all of us. As I am listening to a astrological read for the lunar full moon eclipse coming up in a few days and how vibrant the energy will be. She is stating with all of the great energy don't over do it due to all of the great results this eclipse will bring. I am here to say that this is aligning with everyone who has a creative spark and how and where that will lead you. She also just made a good point, she said the root word of wealthy is well. So, it's about the well being of it all and that will allow space for positive results everywhere. I have had some great results in my life many great lessons in my life and I am in this vibe now where I am looking to create many more great results from all of my great endeavors that I have going on in my life. Picking my pen back up four days later I had some good results this evening after cleaning. All three of my children stayed overnight away from home, so, I am able to keep a clean home for another whole day. That is a great result considering how it all happened. That's just it, It just happened Be Chill Be You and the Rest is the Result...5.18.21

PERSEVERANCE

(EB...BFF INSPIRED)

Is literally the definition of me. I have never stopped, I never have been stopped or have given up. I always made sure I kept my vision and was able to see that light at the end of my tunnel So, all of my life I always knew I was suppose to help heal the world. Make it a better place for you and for me and the entire Human Race Nobody said that better than the man with the greatest albums in the world Michael Jackson. However, the case I always knew that one way or another my voice and ideas would be projected throughout to the world one way or another and I have helped many just by living day to day and helping with issues when I can. So, I felt like with this book how many different kind of people could I help but I must persevere through and complete otherwise they're just words sitting in a book collecting dust. What a waste of talent that would be, so, always think about not only how one thing or the next affects you but how it could affect the next person, but how will it help if they never come into contact with you. Well, this is my way of thinking changing the world is done one person and one day at a time so I must try with all of my soul to spread my abundance of good vibes around so more will want to Perservere..5.18.21

BOUNDARIES

Are set by people who have respect for themselves others and properties of whomever. I must say that it is very coincidental that this is the word that I have for today. See the last twenty entries were just words that were pre placed for the titles, so, boundaries was already here on the page and my situation this morning with my dear sweetheart was concentrated around boundaries and respect. Last night he said something that didn't sit well with me and I knew he was playing so I didn't address it at that moment for I didn't want to cause any static at that moment and I went to sleep on it and woke up feeling the same way about it so when he called me this morning right after I say HEY, I addressed the comment and how it made me feel even though I knew he was only playing it was offensive to me. So as an adult no matter who you are dealing with, if you feel disrespected by anyone at anytime in your life you should address it especially if it's a close so called love based relationship. Because if it goes unchecked the scenario could arise again and again and now when you decide to finally say something the other party is totally confused because the boundaries weren't set in the very beginning. So, it is important to speak up for yourself. We are all different, nobody is perfect but we can definitely Respect one another and their Boundaries!!!

OPPORTUNITIES

Come and go daily if you take the moment to recognize what goes on in front of you. The other day I skipped over this word thinking I didn't have anything interesting or intriguing to converse about. That was really not the case at all, I just was being lazy, not wanting to tap into the word and think about it for a minute. Well, I came back to it a day or two later ready to explain how I see every moment in life as an opportunity, and how to grow from it. Opportunities are all around, I like to use opportunities throughout my day to speak upon the goodness that TMH GOD YHWH has done for me and how if you give him a chance and an opportunity to guide you through, how much more fulfilling life can be. There will always be obstacles, hurdles, and mountains to climb. He also always has your back so when you need a change he will put an opportunity before you whether it involves people, money ventures skill related, or just anything really..(stopped writing and picked back up at 6.6.21).. Funny how much space was left and how I decided to go back and read before final proof read and typing it up to get it ready for publishing. Opportunities really do arise overnight. When one door closes another opens and unfortunately, my Nana checked out a week ago and now my time will be freed up enormously. So, she released me and now it's really my time to shine. So, the bittersweet (not sweet with losing her but sweet in getting back to my life) ending is now going to allow the flow of Opportunity!!

INVESTMENTS

Will be beneficial in the long run. Investments usually require some money to start up with the investment and some investments just require love and time. Like relationships require the latter of the two. That is without any doubt that if you lack with those two you aren't investing much into it then. Now here recently I have begun my new adventure and started investing into cryptocurrency. Crypto is a form of currency and it's just like the stock market. You put your money into the market and watch your money either multiple or decrease. Some would never take this route of investing due to the fact that you can loose so easily and all your money can go down the drain but I am a firm believer that those scenarios can arise from any type of investment from personal purchases to businesses. All money that was used can be wasted in one way or the next, that is why you just take a leap of faith and take a chance to see what you end up with or how well the endeavor mapped out. What I'm saying is if it comes to your mind, Go for it! It will more than likely be successful as long as you stay motivated, that comes from being positive and inspired to thrive daily. So, daily you must invest in self so self can stay strong and focused and ready to adjust self and be ready to roll with the flow of how things go and grow because they're Investments bro or sis...ONELV...5.19.21

BREAKTHROUGH

(look back @ entry Alignment, Power, Creation, Breakthrough)

The madness. Breakthrough the pain. Breakthrough straight to greatness for its yours and mine I am on my way, how about you, are you ready too? This mission is not complete just getting my feet wet so I can see how it feels and it's so real, right in the moment, I have no option but to take my leap, full body not just the feet, but I must pace myself so I don't trip on my own feet or drown myself in my own ocean of dreams. But the time is certainly now. Doors really close right in your face without any warning and if you don't believe a new one is ready to open right after that one you may get stuck in limbo and depression. So, if you must leap you gotta do what you must do to continue on your path of GREATNESS. I'm ready to do it all, write, sing, converse, and many other things even with Covid 19 going around I am not about to be defeated this time around. Even my mind had to have a breakthrough to get to a higher level of thought. When you go through these levels of leveling up in life it's a wonderful time in life and just don't forget to stay humble and grateful because that's what keeps you grounded and ready to elevate and Breakthrough ...6.5.21

COMMITMENT

Means that some of your own time and energy is used toward something and it may not even be for you personally but it is important to you so take it how you receive that. This entry word is beyond easy for me. Why, you ask? Well, I have so many commitments its sometimes overwhelming. Overwhelming only due to the amount of time that is given in one day and by me being only one person that has so many responsibilities which are equally considered commitments to me, so yeah, so much to do in a day and if that's everyday and in which this case my case, yes, everyday, so yeah, you now can maybe see how overwhelming could be the word to sum up how my commitments leave me feeling by the end of the day, not always of course but when I add in a few extra challenges onto my already big list , that is usually when that feeling comes over me. I am forever and always and first and foremostly always committed to the Love and Power of The Most High God and I pray that you too commit yourself today to him if you haven't. He is not hard to find and I do not believe in coincidences if your eyes read it and you feel it, the message was meant for you at this time in your life. Remember we are all energy waiting to connect to the next form of energy. The only man I have been involved with is definitely someone I enjoy spending my time with so I guess that makes it a commitment.

VICTORY

Is closer than close with the date being the 29th of July its been 2 months since I have lost my grandmother whom was a very influential character in the developmental construct of my very own lifestyle and approach to life today. I love and miss her daily. So, as I sit in my work chair and turned on my cool vibes to groove a lil bit and then I immediately wanted to start writing and now I'm singing. Praise TMH God of All Times YHWH. I Love HIM with my Whole Life. In that love and knowing he loves me and the great relationship I have and hold so dear and true is Victory to me alone Honestly!! I could die today just knowing that I still crave the victory of the 3D world with the accolades, achievements and all of those great things but the most important achievement for me isn't being able to finish nor being able to publish this book, but finishing this book up with the third to the last word being VICTORY and being able to share with you the reader, the world, my extended family, how important God the ALMIGHT TRULY IS and how the VICTORY ALL GOES TO HIM because without him we don't have the opportunity to be VICTORIOUS… LOVE ALWAYS!!…ONELV FROM: ME,CRECHE

ACCOMPLISHMENT

Is an excellent display of finalizing. So many different ones throughout our lives. From the beginning of the time of our entrance into the existence of habitating space on this green earth. Birth is an accomplishment for the child and the parent(s). Interesting how I picked up this book on the same day where the date matched the first date we had for the closing on my first home purchase. That is a major accomplishment and so this entry is the second to the last entry and the date is (JANUARY 27TH 2022 and my last entry was written on MAY 14,2021…I stated before.. I pre title before I get to the entry page. And sometimes I move around and not in order page by page) so you may notice the date is well after the last entry date. So, know you aren't tripping when you see the dates ☺ That just means you are detailed and or really into my writings, "THANK YOU" FOR READING. More to come Volumes 2 through 4 atleast, so keep an eye or two out for more. So, stay grounded and focused in your life. Get as close as you can with TMH GOD YHWH he will protect you and be the only GPS you will ever need. I pray that these books inspire other to express themselves and make new accomplishments to add to your list of greatness. Don't stop thriving, Don't stop reaching, Don't stop reading, Don't let anyone stop your motion. Keep moving Forward because that is all you can do. MOVE FORWARD IN CONFIDENCE, GRACE, AND A HEART FULL OF THANKFULNESS AND YOU SHALL ACCOMPLISH…LOVE, ME

INSPIRATIONS

Come in many forms but, this one particularly inspired me to write this book in this entry format. The next entries that will be after this are 4 of 14 that came from one night of writing for an mid- term final. It was a simple assignment. We had to fill up a small 8 sheet front back totaling 16 pages composition or examination book. So, for me since I love writing I just went with what came to my mind at the time to finish quickly. Here recently before I even was mid-way with writing this in this composition book my daughter read to me aloud the entries so I could hear what my own work sound like (14 years ago approx) to me writing this, wow, one of them made me cry because it further inspired me and also confirmed that I was exactly on the correct path of changing the Universe one person at a time 1LOVE..YHWH RULES AND HE LOVES!! I HOPE AND PRAY THAT I AND WE(THE ENTRIES) HAVE BEEN TRU INSPIRATIONS LOVE ME 😊

GHETTOISIM

What really defines ghetto? Ghetto is a strong word to me. Nowadays all kinds of things can be considered as ghetto. I find that really weird. Most of the time you hear of people being ghetto. Also most of the time these people are usually black. Well, that bothers me only because any body can be ghetto. It is true, only because ghetto has so many different meanings. To me ghetto does not mean anything negative. When you speak of being ghetto, I think of the soul of it all. In most ghettos you find black people some doing good and some doing not so good. The point I am trying to make is some people in the "hood" stand strong and enjoy that title of being ghetto and live everyday life. In their everyday life they live like everyone else and participate in all kinds of activities. Now the only way an outsider will be able to know of their ghettoness would be if they portrayed it more than the usual. Example of that would be (huge bangle earrings, funky color hair, or last but never least speaking EBONICS ☺) see but to some in the ghetto that do that everyday, they love it and it also has a name. That name would be "GHETTOFABULOUS" It is cool to be Ghettofabulous sometimes but real people from the hood that represent the hood to the fullest do not mind being ghettofabulous everyday. Now, I could go on and on about the ghettoness in everybody and try to break it all down. So since I am not going to break it all down let me just make one or two more little points. Like I said in the beginning anybody can be ghetto it is all in how you carry yourself. Also if you are happy with how yourself without the next man questioning your actions, carry on. I have no problem with any-one who wants to be ghetto. Man I grew up in the ghetto, Well Inglewood, its considered ghetto to some and home to others. I have seen both sides of the road so, I can call Inglewood a ghetto. Compared to Yorba Linda where I went to school and lived for 5 years. Oh yes, Inglewood is definitely ghetto. So, I guess that makes me ghetto as well. Well, you can call me what you like. I know what and who I am and my name is Creche some would even say my name is Ghetto but if they knew anything, it is a French word. So, basically what I am saying is, Ghetto is really whatever you want it to be, so ghetto can be good, bad, krazy, or down right degrading. It on depends how you take it, So, are you ghetto? 😊

LOVE

Love is a powerful thing. You know most people love but some will tell you they don't love at all. I find that kind of hard to believe. We all have hearts filled with emotions. Love being one of them. When we are born we love our mothers more than anything. Oh we love our fathers too, but its this connection from hearing our mothers heartbeat. That strong heartbeat kept us going until we discovered another love. Puppy love, that is the love we all wish we could see again. I mean that phase of life no the actual person ☺. Well, anyways, yes, that puppy love was exciting. You would go to school everyday just to see that special somebody. If you were lucky the first relationship lasted more than a month. If it didn't it is okay. You weren't necessarily down the road for destruction. Then when you got into High School, you were for sure that the sweetheart of yours was going to be your future spouse. Oh, if love was that easy. Well for some it worked out but not for me and many others. I must admit though High School love was pretty fun. No details, sorry, but I can tell you that when you do find the right one you will definitely know it. The sun is shining and it is night. Do you get my drift? Whoa, drift. How old do I sound? Well, I am old enough to be in love.

LEARNING A LANGUAGE

English is fairly easy when you think about it, only because we speak it. Yet, some people will not learn the language. Now I heard that English is the hardest language to learn. I do not agree with that at all. I have taken 3 other languages and they were all more difficult than English. I took German " Duetch" French "Francais" and Japanese, and that did not last long, maybe a week. I would have to say Japanese was the hardest language ever. Especially for someone who cannot draw a simple stick house. So, yeah, English, the hardest language I doubt it. English words kind of look like Spanish word and some French words but not that many. So our language is pretty straight forward and Spanish and French are a little backwards. Well not backwards but a little rearranged. So, why do we have to learn Spanish to accommodate the Spanish speaking people who live here. I do not think that is fair. Don not get my wrong or anything. I love the culture and the people, I have Mexican Indian heritage within me..However, as I was saying I think they should learn English. I am talking about the elders who do not want to learn it and want someone Spanish speaking to help them. Well, like I said I don't think it is fair, but I want to get paid well, so that is why Spanish 1 is one of my classes.

FRIENDS

Why do we have friends? Why do we have friends that are so much alike? Why do we have friends who may argue and fight? The reason is unknown but I will set this tone. It is all in love. I hold no grudge I may get mad but in a few seconds I'll be glad. Glad that I even have friends to cherish and to hold because some are out there in the cold with no friends to call or to even go play some ball. It is really important to me to keep all friends you see. Even the ones who think they are way too super "OG"(Gangsta) or the ones who know they are too cool. I know Che's no fool. I am a child of God and I love everybody regardless of their downfalls or mishaps. I am not really trying to rap or maybe I am I just really want to get my words across man. I just saw a movie that mad me cry and just heard a shot. That gunshot is going to make his friend cry. So all I am trying to say is life and friends are necessary and important, so take it in stride go take a ride, call a friend and tell them how much you love them or having them around, and simply just for being a friend.

THANK YOU

I really do appreciate you for purchasing and reading my book. This was always my dream and you are apart of that dream as well, you actually purchased it and read it. How awesome is that? VERY, AND THAT'S A FACT!! Take care and Enjoy life to the Fulliest!!! Love Me Cre'Che. :☺